But all things th

are made manifest by the Light.

Ephesians 5:13

Bride of
HEAVEN
Pride of
HELL

Bride of Heaven
Pride of Hell

Ray Comfort

BRIDGE-LOGOS Publishers
North Brunswick, NJ

Bride of Heaven, Pride of Hell
Ray Comfort copyright © 1996

ISBN 0-88270-733-7
Library of Congress Catalog Card number: pending

Ray Comfort
P.O. Box 1172
Bellflower, CA 90706

Published by:
Bridge-Logos Publishers
1300 Airport Road, Ste. E
North Brunswick, NJ 08902

Printed in the United States of America
January 1992, October 1993, October 1996.

Cover design: Erik Hollander
Model for cover illustration: Nada Salloum

In memory of Scott Solomon,
a "good soldier of Jesus Christ."

Special thanks to Kristin Kline,
Hollee Chadwick-Loney, Daniel Comfort,
and my wife Sue, for
their editorial assistance.

The road to Hell is paved with
lack of knowledge.

CONTENTS

FOREWORD

It was the late 1970's. As I sat on a plane awaiting take-off, I looked at the seat pocket in front of me and saw a two-inch square piece of paper sitting precariously by itself on top of the pocket. Obviously, it had torn away from somebody's newspaper as it was pulled out. I leaned forward, took hold of the piece of paper and said in semi-jest, "Could be a word from the Lord." My eyes widened as I stared at the words, *"I have many things to say to you, but ye cannot bear them*--John 16:12."

I didn't doubt what I read, but I had no idea what it meant that I couldn't "bear" what God wanted to show me. Looking back over the years, I now understand what it means. The Greek word for "bear" is *bastazo*, and means to "endure, declare and receive."

One year later, I went into the deepest, darkest, most frightening experience of my life. It lasted for three years, and I took another five years to recover from it. That terrible experience (see my book, *Springboards For Powerful Preaching*, pages 59-76), left me with a broken spirit. It left me at a point where I could receive, endure and declare the many things spoken of. This book is about those, "many things."

Mantle *n*. 1. A loose and usually sleeveless garment worn over other garments.

1
Polishing Off Patients

For several months, the nurses at the Pelonomi Hospital, in Free State, South Africa, were baffled to find a dead patient in the same bed every Friday morning. There was no apparent cause for any of the deaths, and extensive checks on the air conditioning system, and a search for possible bacterial infection, failed to reveal any clues. Obviously, something was terribly wrong.

However, further inquiries revealed the cause of the deaths. It seems that every Friday morning a cleaner would enter the ward, remove the plug that powered the patient's life support system, plug her floor polisher into the vacant socket, then go about her business. When she had finished her chores, she would plug the life support machine back in and leave, unaware that the patient was now dead. She could not, after all, hear the screams of the patient over the whirring of her polisher.

For some time, many have been baffled by a comparable mystery. In 1991, a major denomination in the United States disclosed that during the previous year, they obtained an incredible 294,784 decisions for Christ. But they could only find 14,337 in fellowship (*American Horizons*, March/April 1993 Vol. 2, Number 2). *That means there were 280,447 decisions that couldn't be accounted for*. After extensive inquiries, authorities failed to reveal any clues as to why this happened. The National Director of Home Missions could only say, "Something is wrong!"

These statistics are not confined to that denomination (as we will look at further in this publication), but are in line with the rest of the Church's evangelism, which averages an 80-90% fall away rate. The "loss" is far more than one "patient" once a week. The life's plug is being pulled out, but many are diligently carrying on with their evangelistic work, completely oblivious to what is really happening. In addition, most pastors will tell you that something is wrong in the pews. The average church can only boast of a small percentage of its congregation as having a zeal for God reminiscent of the Church of the Book of Acts. The typical church has only about 20% of the people doing 80% of the work. That same percentage includes the ones who tithe regularly, support prayer meetings, and reach out to the lost. The rest, for some reason, don't.

Statistical Inconsistency

When Jesus gave His disciples the Parable of the Sower, they lacked understanding as to its meaning: "And He said to them, 'Do you not understand this parable? How then will you understand all parables?'" (Mark 4:13). *In other words, the parable of the sower is the key to unlocking the mysteries of all the other parables*. If any message comes from the Parable of the Sower, it is the fact that when the gospel is preached, *there are true and false conversions*. This parable speaks of the thorny ground, the stony ground, and the good soil hearer--the genuine and the false converts.

Once that understanding has been established, then the light of perception begins to dawn on the rest of what Jesus said in parables about the Kingdom of God. If someone doesn't grasp the principle of the true and false being alongside each other, they will be in the dark about almost everything Jesus taught, because He only taught in parables (see Matthew 13:34). The fact that the true and false converts sit alongside each other rings true in many of the other parables, such as the story of the wheat and tares (see Matthew 13:24-30). We need not stay in the realm of conjecture with this, because Jesus gave the interpretation Himself (see Matthew 13:36-43). He said that He was the one who sowed the good seed--the good seed are the children of the Kingdom.

Jesus Himself plants us in the field of the world. Every person who becomes a Christian must be born of His Spirit. In fact, if they are not planted by the Lord, they are not Christians (see Romans 8:9). The tares ("a poisonous grass, almost indistinguishable from wheat" *Unger's Bible Dictionary*, Page 1145) are the children of the wicked one. They have been "sown" by the devil alongside the wheat to a point where the servants of the Lord are told that they won't even discern the difference between the true and the false (see Matthew 13:29). Then in verse 41, we see the actual contrast between the two. The tares are those that do "iniquity" (lawlessness). We have here the true and false converts, side by side, with the false convert continuing to break the Ten Commandments.

Then, after the wheat and tares, Jesus gave the dragnet parable:

> Again, the Kingdom of Heaven is like a dragnet, that was cast into the sea, and gathered some of every kind, which, when it was full, they drew to shore; and sat down, and gathered the good into vessels, but threw the bad away. So it will be at the end of the age. The angels will come forth, and separate the wicked from among the just, and cast them into the furnace of fire. There will be wailing and gnashing of teeth. Jesus said to them, "Have you understood all these things?" They say to Him, "Yes, Lord."
>
> (Matthew 13:47-51)

Notice the good fish and the bad fish were in the net together. The world is not caught in the dragnet of the Kingdom of Heaven. They remain in the world. The "fish" who are caught, are those who respond to the gospel--the evangelistic "catch." Then, the good (true converts) and the bad (false converts) remain side by side within the net of the Church until the time of judgment.

The parables Jesus gave are full of references to the spurious convert. For instance: Matthew 22:10: "So those servants went out into the highways, and gathered together all whom they found, both bad and good: and the wedding hall was filled with guests."

This was the story of the man without a wedding garment. Notice again the "bad" were "gathered" with the good--the true and the false. This man was someone the servants had brought in from the highways for the marriage feast. He had obviously been gathered evangelistically. He thought he was a guest within the Kingdom of God, but he was not. His error was that he did not have a robe of righteousness, and was therefore never a Christian. Unbelievers are called unbelievers because they don't believe. This man did believe. He believed he was saved, but he was not.

If there is no such thing as a false conversion, why did Paul command believers to examine themselves and see if they were "in the faith?" (see 2 Corinthians 13:5).

Look at this disturbing verse in Luke 8:16

Polishing Off Patients

Jesus said, "No man, when he hath lighted a candle, covereth it with a vessel, or putteth it under a bed; but setteth it on a candlestick, that they which enter may see the light." (KJV) This would seem to make reference to the fact that if you are saved, you will therefore be bright enough to let your light shine. Then He spoke of Judgment Day when everything will be brought out into the open: "For nothing is secret, that will not be revealed; nor anything hidden, that will not be made known and come to light. Therefore take heed how you hear. For whoever has, to him more will be given; and whoever does not have, even what he seems to have will be taken from him" (Luke 8:18).

Do you see the word "seems?" These verses are disturbing only in the light of what we see within the contemporary Church. After many years of probing the Body of Christ internationally and transdenominationally to see its state of health, I know that there are many who *seem* to have Jesus Christ, but the Day of Judgment will show the full meaning of the word.

If all is well within the church of America, there is a glaring statistical inconsistency. In 1991, the Graduate School of the City University of New York conducted a poll which indicated that six out of seven Americans identify themselves as Christians. Most who know the Lord would dismiss the statistic, realizing that many of those surveyed would consider a "Christian" to be a non-Moslem or non-Buddhist, etc. However, another poll conducted around the same time is not so easy to dismiss. The Barna Research Institute said that 62% of Americans say they have a "relationship with Jesus Christ that is meaningful to them." Yet, a Gallup Poll, also taken around the same time, revealed something interesting about a special group of 6-10% of Americans who say they are Christians. This is what Mr. Gallup said of them:

> These people are a breed apart . . . they are more tolerant of people of diverse backgrounds. They are involved in charitable activities. They are involved in practical Christianity. They are absolutely committed to prayer.

That sounds like *normal* biblical Christianity. If the 6-10% live like that, then the other 52-56% don't. They are people who say that Jesus is meaningful to them, but they are not a "breed apart." Neither are they involved in good works, nor are they tolerant of others, or involved in practical Christianity or committed to prayer. *That means there are up to 142,000,000 people in America who insinuate that they belong to Jesus Christ, but whose lives don't match their claims.* Surveys show that 90% of the United States prays, but 87% do not believe in all of the Ten Commandments. A massive 92% own a Bible, but only 11% read it daily. Then we are told that 91% lie regularly at work or home, 86% lie regularly to parents and 75% lie regularly to friends (*The Day America Told the Truth*), and according to the Roper Organization, 61% believe that "premarital sex is not morally wrong."

When I find myself in a hotel, I usually channel-surf in an effort to find something wholesome. This often means crossing the polluted and shark-infested waters of MTV. If anything epitomizes this foul-mouthed, sexually perverted, depraved, blasphemous and rebellious generation, it is MTV. In December of 1995, the *Youth Leader Magazine* said: "More Christian teens watch MTV each week (42%) than non-Christians (33%), according to a Barna Research Group survey of evangelical teens." Then the article went on to quote Barna as saying that their survey showed that of these same teens, 65% said they prayed daily, 72% believed the Bible and that

over a three month period 66% had lied to a
parent or teacher, 55% had sex, 55% had cheated
in an exam and 20% got drunk or had used illegal
drugs.

A Christian youth leader was interviewed
recently on a popular national radio program. In
it, he spoke with great concern of the fact that
young people were "leaving the Church in
droves." Then he cited the number one reason
they were turning their backs on God. His survey
said it was a "lack of opportunity in the Church,"
inferring that the Church should get its act
together and give young people more opportunity.
Ask any pastor if there is "opportunity" to serve
within his church and he will no doubt tell you of
the lack of people to teach Sunday school, of
people to clean the restrooms, to visit the elderly,
to visit the sick, to go out with the evangelism
team, to clean the church building, etc.

The truth is, if someone is a Judas at heart, he
will find *any* excuse to go back into the world. If
Judas was given a survey form to fill out, no
doubt he would have had many justifications for
his treachery:

1. He was humiliated by Jesus,
   when he suggested giving funds
   to the poor.

2. He felt a deep sense of rejection because he wasn't part of the "inner circle."
3. He needed the money.
4. The Chief Priests made him do it.
5. The devil made him do it.
6. The responsibility of looking after the finances became too much for him.
7. He was abused as a child.
8. He had a betrayal-syndrome.
9. He lacked a father-figure.
10. He didn't think his actions would have the grisly repercussions they had.

In 1996, the Alan Guttmacher Institute in New York conducted a survey which found that "18% of abortion patients describe themselves as born-again or evangelical Christians." (*US News & World Report*, August 19, 1996). That is, nearly one in five of those who murdered their own child, professed faith in Jesus Christ.

In 1994, the Barna Research Group found further evidence that all is not well in the contemporary church. A survey revealed that one in four American adults who said they were "born again," think that Jesus "sinned" while He was on the earth. Think for a moment of the implications of such a warped theology. Here we have "believers" who supposedly confess that "Jesus is Lord," and yet they say that He sinned. That means that the Word of God is inaccurate when it says Jesus "knew no sin" (2 Corinthians 5:21), that He was "in all points tempted as we are, yet without sin" (Hebrews 4:15), and that He "did no sin, neither was guile found in His mouth" (1 Peter 2:22). It means that Jesus wasn't therefore the "spotless Lamb of God" the Scriptures say He was. His sacrifice wasn't perfect, and when God accepted His death as an atonement for our sins, He sanctioned a "contaminated payment" and is therefore corrupt by nature.

Sadly, the only logical conclusion we can come to, is to say that these multitudes who profess faith in Jesus, who think they are part of the Church because they have made a decision and therefore profess to be "born again," are in truth, strangers to regeneration.

2
True Happiness

Few could deny that the Church as a whole has fallen short of the ideal we see in the Book of Acts. This has happened because the enemy has very subtly taken the focus off our message. Instead of preaching the good news that individuals can be made righteous in Christ *and escape the wrath to come*, the gospel has degenerated into the pretext that we can be made happy in Christ *and escape the hassles of this life*. One tragic result of this is that it has diffused the Church of a sense of urgency.

One of America's largest publishers recently put out a quality full color publication that epitomized what I am saying. It was entitled, "Is There a Way Out?" Inside it reads:

Everyone is looking for a way out of their problems. There's no easy way out. You won't get respect by joining a gang. You won't find love in the back seat of a car. You'll never find success by dropping out of school. And the chances are about one million to one that you'll win the lottery. If you're *really* serious about making your life better, then try God's way. God gets right to the source of most of our problems: sin.

If the way out of problems is to become a Christian, the apostle Paul never found it. The first thing Jesus said of him was that He would show him "how great things he must suffer for My name's sake" (Acts 9:16). Three times Paul was beaten with rods, once he was stoned, three times he suffered shipwreck, a night and a day he spent in the sea. There were times when Paul was so unhappy, he wanted to die (see 2 Corinthians 1:8).

The Bible says, "*All* who live godly in Christ Jesus *shall* suffer persecution" (2 Timothy 3:12, italics added, KJV). It says we enter the Kingdom of God through much tribulation (see Acts 14:22), and that we were appointed to afflictions (see 1 Thessalonians 3:3).

True Happiness

The Scriptures speak of the Christian suffering "tribulation." They speak of "fiery trials," being "partakers of Christ's sufferings," of the "afflictions of the gospel," and of the "fellowship of His sufferings." Paul said he suffered the loss of *all* things for the sake of the gospel.

Jesus never hinted that following Him was a way out of problems. He said if we followed Him we would be reviled, persecuted, hated, and all manner of evil would be said against us falsely, for His sake. He warned that we would have to take up our cross daily, deny ourselves and follow Him, saying, "In the world you shall have tribulation" (John 16:33), and even that we may be called to die for our faith (see Luke 21:16).

Neither did godly men and women of past ages find that godly living was a way out of problems. They were "stoned, they were sawn in two, were tempted, were slain with the sword: they wandered about in sheepskins and goatskins; being destitute, afflicted (and) tormented" (Hebrews 11:37).

Well-known author and Bible teacher John MacArthur said, "To tell an unbeliever that God has a wonderful plan for his life can be seriously misleading." (*John MacArthur New Testament Commentary*, Matthew 19).

It would seem at first sight that, in their zeal to

27

reach the lost, modern preachers are propagating a misrepresentation of the truth of the gospel of Jesus Christ.

There is Another Explanation

If however, those who say "Jesus solves problems," were "converted" under the sound of the same gospel they propagate, and did not repent themselves, then there may be some truth in what they are saying. If they continue to live in lawlessness, then they don't have a struggle with the world, the flesh, and the devil. They are friends of the world. They flow *with* it rather than *against* it, and therefore don't have "tribulation" in it. They don't "live godly in Christ Jesus," and so they don't "suffer persecution." They are not hated for His name's sake because their lives are no different from those who are in the world. They live in the flesh, and therefore don't struggle to deny the flesh.

They also don't wrestle against the devil. In fact, he will be pleased with what he sees. They joined the fellowship of the Church, they enjoy the music, the worship, the friendship, and the many other benefits of modern Christianity, including what they think is assurance of everlasting life. They *have* found happiness in their new lifestyle.

But here's the double tragedy from such error. When the Church declares the message that "Jesus gives happiness," it restricts its field of evangelistic endeavor to those in society who will be interested--*those who are not happy* . . . those with alcohol, drug, marriage, personality and financial problems.

These "problem" people don't hear the message of sin, righteousness, and judgment, with the command to repent and flee from the wrath which is to come. Instead they hear that Jesus is the answer to their marriage, alcohol, drug, and financial problems. He is the One who can fill the God-shaped vacuum in their lives. They therefore fail to repent (because they haven't been told to), they have a false conversion (see Mark 4:16-17), and don't become new creatures in Christ. They do "name the name of Christ," but they don't "depart from iniquity." Rather, they bring their sins *and their problems* into the Church. This has the sad effect of:

1. Wearing out the pastor. Instead of being able to fully give himself to feeding the flock of God in the capacity of a shepherd, he finds himself forever counseling those who are "hearers of the Word only and not doers."

2. Tragically, the happiness gospel then has the laborers (who are already few in number) tied up in the function of being counselors and propping people up, when these problem people need neither counsel or prop-up--they need repentance.

J.I. Packer speaks of the many problems plaguing the modern church. Then he says these insightful words: "This complex phenomenon, to which many factors have contributed; but, if we go to the root of the matter, we shall find that these perplexities are all ultimately due to our having lost our grip on the biblical gospel. Without realizing it, we have during the past century bartered that gospel for a substitute product which, though it looks similar enough in points of detail, is as a whole a decidedly different thing. Hence our troubles." (*Introductory Essay*, J.I. Packer, p. 2, Chapel Library).

In a publication called, "What Do You Want From Life?" the conclusion is drawn that we all want to be happy. Despite the list of things cited-- sex, money, friends, fame, love, etc., the question is: Can we be *truly* and *continually* happy? The answer is of course that knowing Jesus produces "ultra happiness . . . your happiest moment magnified a million times over."

Not many would see that there is anything wrong with this publication. However, the call of the gospel is universal, and not confined to the unhappy "hurting" world, as it is so often promoted. The gospel is a promise of *righteousness*, not a promise of happiness, and it therefore may also be offered to those who are *enjoying* the "pleasures of sin for a season." Before my conversion, I was very happy, content, satisfied, cheerful, thankful, and joyful. I was loving life, and living it to the fullest. *Therefore, I was not a candidate for the modern gospel*. However, when I was confronted by the spirituality of God's Law (the Ten Commandments--the word "Law" is capitalized to separate it from civil law), and understood that "riches profit not on the Day of wrath, but *righteousness* delivers from death," I saw my need of the Savior.

Let me repeat: because of the belief that the chief end of the gospel is man's happiness on earth, rather than his righteousness, many fail to see its God-given intention. They think the gospel is only for those who lack money, those who are brokenhearted by life's difficulties--those who are the problem people in society. The belief is further pervaded through popular worship choruses which have splendid melodies, but carry this message: "Heartaches, broken people, ruined lives is why You died on Calvary . . . " Evangelistic outreaches are billed as taking the Good News to the "hurting and the needy." Again, the gospel is not confined to the "hurting" people with ruined lives and heartaches. Both hurting *and happy* people need to be shown their sinful state before God, so they will seek after the righteousness which is in Christ.

Let me further illustrate this common misunderstanding, by quoting from another modern publication (I am in no way questioning the sincerity of the author):

"You will desire to be where the Lord is. And He spends His time with those who hurt. At the beginning of His ministry, Jesus quoted Isaiah to describe the work He was called to do: (then the author quotes Luke 4:18-19, and continues) . . . *thus the more you go after God, the deeper you will move into a world filled with hurting people.*"

True Happiness

In the passage cited by the author (Luke 4:18-19), Jesus said, "The Spirit of the Lord is upon me, because He has anointed me to preach the gospel to the poor; He has sent me to heal the brokenhearted, to preach deliverance to the captives, and recovery of sight to the blind, to set at liberty them that are oppressed, to preach the acceptable year of the Lord."

Here Jesus gives us a summation of who the gospel is for. The Good News is for:

1. The poor
2. The brokenhearted
3. The captives
4. The blind
5. The oppressed.

A quick study will show that Jesus is not necessarily speaking of those who lack financial resources when He speaks of the "poor." The word means, "meek, humble, lowly"--the "poor in spirit" (see Matthew 5:3). These are the blessed ones to whom the Kingdom of God belongs. The *poor* are those who know that they are destitute of righteousness. The following statement is what Matthew Henry said of the verse: "To whom was He to preach: to the *poor*; to those that were *poor in this world*; to those that were *poor in spirit*, to the meek and humble, and those that were truly sorrowful for sin." (*The Matthew Henry Commentary*, Zondervan Publishing House, p. 1425).

When He speaks of the "brokenhearted," He doesn't mean those unhappy people whose hearts are aching because they have been jilted by a sweetheart, but those who are contrite, like Peter and Isaiah, those sorrowing for sin.

Listen to the respected Bible commentator once again: "For He was sent to heal the brokenhearted, to give peace to those who were troubled and humbled for sins, and to bring them to rest who were weary and heavy-laden, and the burden of guilt and corruption" (Ibid.).

The *captives* are those "taken captive by the devil to do his will" (2 Timothy 2:26).

The *blind* are those "whom the god of this world has blinded to the light of the glorious gospel of Christ" (2 Corinthians 4:4).

The *oppressed* are those who are oppressed by the devil (see Acts 10:38).

The gospel of grace is for the humble, not the proud. God resists the proud, and gives grace to the humble (see James 4:6; 1 Peter 5:5). "Everyone who is proud in heart is an abomination to the Lord" (Proverbs 16:5). He has put down the mighty from their seats, and exalted them that are of low degree. He sets on high those who are lowly, and those who mourn are lifted to safety (see Job 5:11). God looks to the man that is poor and of a contrite spirit, and trembles at His Word (see Isaiah 66:2). Only the sick need a physician, and those who are convinced of the disease will appreciate and appropriate the cure.

How can we therefore most effectively present the gospel? This we will look at in the next chapter.

3

Making Grace Amazing

The initiator of the comprehensive study, which found that over 260,000 converts couldn't be accounted for, concluded his commentary by saying, "Something is wrong." It has been wrong for nearly one hundred years of evangelism, since the Church forsook the key to the sinner's heart. When it set aside the Law of God (the Ten Commandments) in its function to convert the soul (see Psalm 19:7), it removed the sinner's means of seeing his need of God's forgiveness. Of course, the Law cannot justify us, it wasn't given for that purpose. No one can be right with God through keeping the Law.

Romans 5:20 tells us why it "entered" the scene: "Moreover the Law entered, that the offense might abound. But where sin abounded, grace did much more abound." When sin abounds, grace "much more" abounds; and according to Scripture, the thing that makes sin abound is the Law.

We can see the work of God's Law illustrated in civil law. Watch what often happens on a freeway when there is no visible sign of the law. See how motorists transgress the speed limit. It seems that the law has forgotten to patrol this part of the freeway. Besides, you are only transgressing the law by 15 MPH, and you are not the only one doing it.

Notice what happens when the law enters down the fast lane with red lights flashing. Your heart misses a beat. You no longer feel secure in the fact that other motorists are also speeding. You know that you are *personally* as guilty as the next guy, and *you* could be the one the law pulls over. Suddenly, your "mere" 15 MPH transgression doesn't seem such a small thing after all; it seems to abound.

Look at the freeway of sin. The whole world naturally goes with the flow. Who hasn't had an "affair" (or desired to) at some time or another? Who in today's society doesn't tell the occasional "white" lie? Who doesn't take something that belongs to someone else, even if it's just "white collar" crime? They know they are doing wrong, but their security is in the fact that so many others are just as guilty, if not worse. It seems God has forgotten all about sin and the Ten Commandments--"He has said in his heart, 'God has forgotten; He hides His face; He will never see it'" (Psalm 10:11).

Now watch the Law enter with red lights flashing. The sinner's heart is stopped. He lays his hand upon his mouth. He examines the speedometer of his conscience. Suddenly, it shows him the measure of his guilt in a new light--the light of the Law. His sense of security in the fact that there are multitudes doing the same thing becomes irrelevant, because every man will give an account of *himself* to God. Sin not only becomes personal, it seems to "abound." His mere lust becomes *adultery of the heart* (see Matthew 5:27-28); his white lie, *false witness* (see Revelation 21:8); his own way becomes *rebellion*; his hatred, *murder* (see 1 John 3:15); his "sticky" fingers make him a *thief*--"Moreover the Law entered, that the offense might abound." Without the Law entering, sin is neither personal, nor is it veritable: "For without the Law, the sense of sin is inactive" (Romans 7:8b, *The Amplified Bible*).

It was the "Commandment" that showed Paul sin in its true light, that it is "exceedingly sinful" (see Romans 7:13). Paul spoke from his own experience because he sat at the feet of Gamaliel, the great "teacher of the Law" and therefore saw sin in its true colors.

The Offense and the Foolishness of the Cross

According to Romans 3:20, "The real function of the Law is to make men recognize and be conscious of sin, not mere perception, but an acquaintance with sin which works towards repentance" (*The Amplified Bible*).

To illustrate this point: Imagine if I said to you, "I have some good news for you! *Someone has just paid a $25,000 speeding fine on your behalf!*" You would probably answer me with some cynicism in your tone, "What are you talking about? *I don't have a $25,000 speeding fine!*"

Your reaction would be quite understandable. If you don't know you have broken the law in the first place, the good news of someone paying a fine for you won't be good news, it will be foolishness to you. My insinuation of unlawful activity will even be offensive to you.

But if I was to put it this way it may make more sense: "Today, the law clocked you traveling at 55 MPH in an area designated for a blind childrens' convention. You totally ignored ten clear warning signs saying that the maximum speed was 15 MPH. What you did was *extremely* dangerous. The fine is $25,000 or imprisonment. The law was about to take its course when someone you don't even know stepped in and paid the fine for you. *You are very fortunate.*"

Can you see that telling you the good news of the fine being paid, without telling you that you have broken the law first, will leave you thinking the "good news" is nothing but nonsense? To make known your transgression actually *gives sense* to the good news. An unclouded explanation of the law, *so that you can clearly see your violation*, helps you understand and also *appreciate* the good news.

In the same way, to tell someone the good news that Jesus died on the Cross for their sins, makes no sense to them: "For the message of the Cross is foolishness to those who are perishing" (1 Corinthians 1:18). Therefore it is also quite understandable for him to say, "What are you talking about? *I haven't got any 'sins.'* I try to live a good life," etc. Your insinuation that he is a sinner, when he doesn't think he is, will be offensive to him.

But those who take the time to follow in the footsteps of Jesus and open up the "spirituality of the Law," carefully explaining the meaning of the Ten Commandments, will see the sinner become *convinced of the Law as a transgressor* (see James 2:9). Once he understands his transgression, the good news will neither be offensive nor foolishness, but the power of God to salvation.

What 'Sin' Are You Talking About?

When David sinned with Bathsheba, he broke all of the Ten Commandments. He coveted his neighbor's wife, lived a lie, stole her, committed adultery, killed her husband, dishonored his parents, and thus dishonored God. So, the Lord sent Nathan the prophet to reprove him.

Notice the order in which the reproof came. Nathan gave David (the shepherd of Israel) a parable about something that he could understand-- sheep. He began with the natural realm, rather than immediately exposing the King's sin. He told a story about a rich man who, instead of taking a sheep from his own flock, killed a poor man's pet lamb to feed a stranger.

David was indignant, and sat up on his high throne of self-righteousness. He revealed his knowledge of the Law by saying that the guilty party would restore fourfold, and that he would die for his crime. Nathan then exposed the king's sin of taking another man's "lamb," saying, "You are the man . . . Why have you despised the commandment of the Lord, to do evil in His sight?" (2 Samuel 12:9). When David cried, "I have sinned against the Lord!" (2 Samuel 12:13), the prophet *then* gave him grace and said, "The Lord has also put away your sin; you shall not die."

Imagine if Nathan, *fearful of rejection*, changed things around a little, and instead told David, "God loves you and has a wonderful plan for your life. However, there is something which is keeping you from enjoying this wonderful plan; it is called 'sin.'"

Imagine if he had glossed over the *personal nature* of David's sin, with a general reference to *all* men having sinned and fallen short of the glory of God. David's reaction may have been, "What *sin* are you talking about?" rather than admit his terrible transgression. Think of it--why should he cry, "*I have sinned against the Lord!*" at the sound of that message? Instead, he may have, in a sincere desire to experience this "wonderful plan," admitted that he, like all men, had sinned and fallen short of the glory of God.

If David had not been made to tremble under the wrath of the Law, the prophet would have removed the very means of producing godly sorrow, which was so necessary for David's repentance. It is "godly sorrow" that works repentance (see 2 Corinthians 7:10). It was the weight of his guilt that caused him to cry out, "*I have sinned against the Lord!*" The Law caused him to labor and become heavy laden; it made him hunger and thirst for righteousness . . . it enlightened him as to the serious nature of sin as far as God was concerned.

Sin is like an onion. Its outer wrapper is a dry and crusty self-righteousness. It is only when its external casing is peeled away that it brings tears to the human eye. The Law peels the onion, and allows contrition.

The Vase

A child broke his father's antique vase, a vase he was forbidden to touch, one that was worth $25,000. However, the child thought the vase was merely worth $2, so he wasn't too concerned. He could easily replace it. It was only when he was later told of its true value . . . $25,000 . . . that he saw the seriousness of his transgression and found a place of sorrow of heart. It was knowledge of the solemn nature of breaking an antique he was told not to touch, that gave him the ability to find a place of sorrow of heart. If he had been left in ignorance as to the value of the vase, he wouldn't have been truly sorry. Would you be upset if you had broken a vase you could easily replace?

The Lawless "God loves you and has a wonderful plan for your life" message doesn't cause the sinner to tremble. It doesn't show him the utterly serious nature of his transgression, so he doesn't find godly sorrow which works repentance.

How true are the words once spoken by Charles Spurgeon, the Prince of Preachers. "The Law serves a most necessary purpose." He also said, "They will *never* accept grace, until they tremble before a just and holy Law." Those who see the role of the Law will be sons of thunder *before* they are the sons of consolation. They know that the shoes of human pride must be removed before sinners can approach the burning bush of the gospel.

Paradox though it may seem, the Law does make grace abound, in the same way darkness makes light shine. It was John Newton, the writer of "Amazing Grace," who said that a wrong understanding of the harmony between Law and grace would produce "error on the left and the right hand." I don't know if any of us could claim to have a better understanding of grace than the one who penned such a hymn.

The world will never clearly see the light of the glorious gospel of Christ, until the blackness of sin is explicitly painted on the canvas of a just and holy Law. When a Christian sees what he has been saved *from*, he will realize what he has been saved *for*. He will have a love for God, because of the unspeakable gift of the Cross. It will be a continual source of joy. Gratitude for grace will motivate him to reach out and do the will of God, to seek and save that which is lost.

4
The Key Was in
the Folding

In the first chapter, we looked at the mass of decisions that disappeared from a major denomination in the United States in 1991. Again, this sad statistic is not confined to that denomination. This tragedy has come about because of two reasons. First, the modern gospel has degenerated into a means of happiness, rather than one of righteousness. Second, we have failed to show the sinner that he is a law-breaker, that he has violated the Law of a Holy God.

When I speak of the use of the Law in evangelism, I am not speaking of a mere casual reference to it, *but as the backbone of the gospel presentation,* because its function is to prepare the heart for grace, as it did for David through Nathan. The Law is the rod and staff of the shepherd to guide the sheep to himself. It is the net of the fisherman, and the hoe of the farmer. It is the ten golden trumpets that prepare the way for the King. The Law makes the sinner thirst for righteousness, that he might live. Its holy light reveals the dust of sin on the table of the human heart, so that the gospel in the hand of the Spirit can wipe it perfectly clean.

He who labors under the conviction of the Law, and is heavy laden under the weight of his sin, greatly appreciates the "rest" of the Savior. He comes by the way of repentance, gladly takes the yoke of Christ, willingly learns of Him Who is meek and lowly of heart, and thus finds "rest to his soul." This is true conversion.

There are, however, many people who seem to stand as testimonies of modern preaching, like the 14,337 who remained in the churches in the survey previously mentioned. They more than likely came into the Church under the message of those who do not use the Law as a schoolmaster to bring sinners to Christ. All these people heard was that Jesus died on the Cross for their sins, and that they would never find true peace until they found peace with God. They were told that they needed to repent and trust Jesus Christ.

Those who preach grace alone look to these many thousands who have remained in fellowship, as clear evidence to justify the presentation of a gospel which makes no reference to the Law.

Mangled Bodies

During a great war there was a man who invented a parachute which was 100% trust-worthy. It made no difference how big or small the person was who used it; it opened every time and got him safely to the ground. The key was in the way it was folded. Every part of the parachute had to be carefully and painstakingly placed in certain positions, following the instructions given by the manufacturer. True, it was somewhat arduous, but it was well worth the effort. It had the effect of making sure that the life of every precious human being who trusted the parachute was being preserved.

Many years after the war began, a group of young men known as "fast-folders," entered the packing room. These men so influenced the workers with their new fast and easy method of folding, they completely ignored the instruction book given by the manufacturer. Production increased greatly and everyone rejoiced that so much time and effort had been saved.

However, as time passed it slowly became evident that something was radically wrong. In fact, a small group of investigators who went to where the parachutes were being used found, to their horror, that *of every ten men who jumped using the new method, nine tragically fell to their deaths*.

The horrible sight of so many mangled and rotting bodies, strewn all over the ground, sickened them. These weren't just faceless customers. These were husbands, fathers, mothers, sons, and daughters . . . cherished human beings who were falling to a needless and terrifying death.

A report was quickly taken back to the fastfolders. Many were heartbroken, and immediately went back to the instruction book and corrected the mistake. With great sobriety and care, they began painstakingly folding each parachute exactly as the book said. Their knowledge of the tragedies made sure they did their job with uncompromising conviction.

Yet, there was resistance from a few. Even though they knew that so many lives were being lost, they still refused to follow the instruction book. Unbelievably, they ignored the mass of mangled and rotting bodies, for which they were directly responsible, and instead *pointed to the ones who had survived their fast-folding, as justification for their method.*

Free From Their Blood

The Church is at war. The battle is for the souls of men and women. Those who have gone before us in past centuries have not had an easy task. Labor in the gospel was often slow and arduous. But they knew *if they followed according to the pattern of God's Word,* with His help, they would eventually deliver men and women from death and Hell. If they sowed in tears, they would reap in joy. They, above all things, wanted to be "true and faithful witnesses." If they preached the whole counsel of God, they would be free from the blood of all men. These ministries, such as that of Wesley, Wycliff, Whitefield, Spurgeon, and others, were greatly effective in reaching the lost. *The key was in the careful and thorough use of the Law to prepare the way for the gospel.*

As time went by, certain men discovered that the message of the gospel could be condensed and presented in a fast and much easier way. The trouble was, this quick and easy method had a number of problems.

First, *its presentation was unbiblical.* It didn't follow the Scriptural example by presenting the balance of Law and grace. Jesus did, but they didn't. He always preached Law to the proud and arrogant, and grace to the meek and the humble (see Luke 10:25; Luke 18:18; Mark 12:28; John 3:3-17). Never once did the Son of God give the good news . . . the Cross . . . grace, and mercy . . . to the proud, the arrogant, or the self-righteous. He followed His Father's example Who resists the proud and gives grace to the humble. Paul did the same, as seen at Athens and on other occasions. Biblical evangelism is *always* "Law to the proud, and grace to the humble." With the Law, we should break the hard heart, and with the gospel, heal the broken one.

Without the Law, there can be no knowledge of sin: "What shall we say then? Is the Law sin? God forbid. Nay, *I had not known sin, but by the Law* . . . For without the Law sin was dead. For I was alive without the Law once: but when the Commandment came, sin revived, and I died" (Romans 7:7-10, italics added, KJV).

The Law was the instrument of the death of the old nature. It made sure that sinners were truly born again, that the Adamic nature was destroyed by nailing it to the Cross. It made certain that the convert was a new creature in Christ.

The Key Was in the Folding

Yet, the new and modern method forsook the Law in its power to convert the soul. It did, however, speed the process of evangelism, making it much easier to get commitments. Also, it stirred less opposition, and it seemed to get results. So everyone rejoiced.

It also failed to mention the fact of Judgment Day. The Bible held forth the great and terrible Day of the Lord *as the very reason* to repent and trust the Savior: "Truly, these times of ignorance God overlooked, but now commands all men everywhere to repent, *because He has appointed a day, on which He will judge the world in righteousness"* (Acts 17:31, italics added). *The new presentation was not faithful to God--it didn't even hint of Judgment Day's approach*. The reason Jesus died on the Cross was to save us from wrath (see 1 Thessalonians 1:10). That is the essence of the message of the gospel, but there wasn't even a mention of Hell's existence. They ripped the heart out of the Body of the gospel. General Booth warned, that in this century, a gospel would be preached which promised Heaven without mentioning Hell. Modern evangelism did just that. Take the time to study closely the contents of the

most popular tract ever printed and see the four
flaws of the Laodicean presentation:

1. No mention of Judgment Day.
2. Not a hint of Hell.
3. No use of the Law of God to
   bring the knowledge of sin.
4. The gospel is held up as a means
   of happiness, rather than a
   means of righteousness.

That is a perfect recipe for a false conversion--
a stony ground hearer. He receives the Word with
joy and gladness, but in a time of tribulation,
temptation, and persecution, he falls away. He is
like the "young man" in Mark 14:51-52, who had
a "linen cloth cast about his naked body." When
persecution came, he cast off his covering, and
fled naked.

God knows that I hesitate to be critical of the
authors of modern literature. They are sincere,
earnest, loving, godly brethren, but their zeal has
lacked knowledge, and the results are a
devastation that cannot be ignored.

In Jeremiah 26, when God told the prophet to

rebuke His people, He warned that he was to speak "all the words that I command you to speak. Do not diminish a word" (vs. 2). Then, when Jeremiah spoke all that the Lord had commanded him, the people seized him and said, "You shall surely die!" (vs. 8). It was the fact of judgment that offended them. We are then told that the princes of Judah sat down at the entry of the "new gate of the Lord's House" (vs. 10).

We have diminished more than one word, and the result has been a new gate in the Lord's House. It is not the straight gate with a narrow way, but a new gate with a broad path. We will look at this in depth later.

All Have Sinned

The modern method also glossed over sin. Probably the mainstay of the mention of sin in modern evangelism is Romans 3:23: "For all have sinned, and come short of the glory of God." On looking at that Scripture, the question I would ask if I was not a Christian is, *"What is meant by 'glory?'"* Often we hear how the word "sin" was shouted during archery, to let the person firing the arrow know that they had fallen short of the target. If I have fallen short of a mark, I should at least desire to know what and where the target is, *to measure how much I have fallen short,* to know whether I should give up or try for another shot.

The Greek word used in the text is *doxa,* which literally means "honor, praise, worship." Humanity has fallen short of the honor, the worship, and the praise of God. We have failed to give our Creator the honor, the worship, and the praise due to Him. We have failed to love God with all of our heart, mind, soul, and strength, which is the essence of the Law (see Mark 12:30). In fact, "all have sinned" comes in the context of Paul saying that the Law has left the whole world guilty before God (see Romans 3:19). By calling "sin!" to a sinner, but failing to tell him anything about the mark he is aiming for, is to let him think that he can still give it his "best shot." However, to display the Law in front of him, is to leave him without hope of ever coming near the mark, so that his only hope will be in the Savior.

The great stones of the Law convinced the adulterous woman, in John, chapter 8, that she needed mercy. She had no other avenue but to fall at the feet of Jesus of Nazareth.

The Key Was in the Folding

An old movie showed an officer of the law entering an illegal gambling casino. The manager asked, "Are you going to speak to the people before you arrest them? *They must have the law spelled out to them so that they will know that what they are doing is wrong.*"

Doesn't that make sense? How on earth are the gamblers going to come peacefully if they don't realize they have broken the law?

5

The Natural Result

With the modern method, the Commandments were dropped as the means of showing what sin was, and because the method failed to give a *reason* for men and women to repent and trust the Savior, the fast and easy presentation had to find one. Why should sinners trust Jesus--to flee to the Savior to escape the wrath of God's Law, and consequently the damnation of Hell? No, the reason given that they should come was to experience a "wonderful new life" which God had for them in Christ. Jesus became a life-improver, even though this was in direct competition with the *Book of Mormon,* which promises "genuine peace and lasting happiness," as does Scientology, New Age, and many other fashionable lifestyles offered by secular society.

Soberly, come with me now to the landing ground on which those fall who "put on the Lord Jesus Christ" using the fast-folding method:

1. In 1990, in a crusade in the U.S., 600 decisions were obtained. No doubt there was much rejoicing. However, 90 days later, follow up workers *couldn't find* even one who was going on in his or her faith. That crusade created 600 "backsliders," or to be more scriptural, "false converts."

2. In 1991, in Cleveland Ohio, in an "Inner City Outreach," rejoicing no doubt tapered when those who were involved in follow up once again couldn't find one of the 400 who had made a decision.

3. In 1985, a four day crusade obtained 217 decisions, but according to a member of the organizing committee, 92% fell away.

4. Charles E. Hackett, the Division of Home Missions National Director for the Assemblies of God in the United States, said, "A soul at the altar does not generate much excitement in some circles because we realize approximately 95 out of every 100 will not become integrated into the church. In fact, most of them will not return for a second visit."

5. In his book, *Today's Evangelism*, Ernest C. Reisinger spoke of an outreach and said, "It lasted eight days, and there were 68 supposed conversions." A month later, not one of the "converts" could be found.

6. In 1991, in Salt Lake City, organizers of a concert encouraged follow up. They said, "Less than 5% of those who respond to an altar call during a public crusade . . . are living a Christian life one year later." In other words, *more than* 95% proved to be false converts.

7. A pastor in Boulder, Colorado, sent a team to Russia in 1991 and attained 2,500 decisions. The next year, they found that only 30 were going on in their faith.

8. In Leeds, England, a visiting U.S. speaker acquired 400 decisions for a local church. However, six weeks later only two were going on, and they eventually fell away.

9. A mass crusade reported 18,000 decisions, yet according to *Church Growth Magazine*, tragically 94% failed to even become incorporated into a local church.

10. Back in November of 1970, a number of churches combined for a convention in Fort Worth, Texas, and secured 30,000 decisions. Six months later, the follow up committee could only find 30 going on in their faith.

11. In 1994, in Sacramento, California, a combined crusade yielded over 2,000 commitments. One church followed up 52 of those decisions and couldn't find one conversion.

12. In August 1996, a leading U.S. denomination published that during 1995 they secured 384,057 decisions, but retained only 22,983 in fellowship. They couldn't account for 361,074 supposed conversions. That's a 94% fall away rate.

13. In Omaha, Nebraska, a pastor of a large church said he was involved with a crusade where 1300 decisions were made, and not even one went on in his or her faith.

14. A pastor, who has traveled to India every year since 1980, told me that he saw 80,000 decision cards stacked in a hut in the city of Rajamundry, the "results" of past evangelistic crusades. But he maintained that one would be fortunate to find even 80 Christians in the entire city.

15. A major Christian television network broadcast an interview with a Russian Christian leader on July 5th, 1996. She said of Russian converts, "Many thousands have received salvation and healing . . . but because of there not being many leaders, not many stayed with their faith."

16. And of course there were the 260,000 false converts created by a major denomination in the United States back in 1991.

These statistics are as rare as hen's teeth. What organizing committee is going to shout from the housetops, that after a mass of pre-crusade prayer, hundreds of thousands of dollars of expenditure, truckloads of follow up, and the use of a big name evangelist, initial wonderful results have all disappeared? Not only would such news be utterly disheartening for all who put so much time and effort into the crusade, *but the committee has no reasonable explanation as to why the massive catch has disappeared*. The statistics are therefore swept under the hushed carpet of discretion.

The following article bravely appeared in a southern California newspaper in July, 1993:

> Crusades don't do as much for non-believers as some might think, said Peter Wagner, professor of church growth at Fuller Theological Seminary in Pasadena. Three percent to 16 percent of those who make decisions at crusades end up responsible members of a church, he said. "That's not counting Christians who recommit their lives."

The Natural Result

These statistics of an 84%-97% fall away rate are not confined to crusades, but are general throughout local church evangelism. The problem is not with the crusades, but with the modern methods and message of evangelism.

Sadly, these are not isolated cases. The mangled bodies of those who are commonly called backsliders, lay strewn around the ground as a disastrous result of modern evangelism.

I can't put into words the utter tragedy of seeing so many spurious converts who have *left* the Church, and the multitudes of false converts that *stay within* the Church. *These things need not be*. We are not talking about "church growth" or mere "statistics," but the salvation of human beings from death and eternal damnation in Hell. We must put a quick end to the fast and easy method, even though it gets rid of the reproach of the gospel and seems to be filling our churches. We must go back to the Instruction Book of God's Word and see what it says. If we say we love the truth, we must speak the truth in love.

Don't be tempted to ignore the disastrous results, and look at those *comparatively* few who are going on in their faith as justification for the method. Remember, for every 1,000 genuine converts *there are as many as 9,000 who lay mangled on the soil of hard hearts, directly as a result of the quick and easy methods of modern Laodicean evangelism.*

A Good Yarn

Have you ever noticed how Jesus used fiery and scathing words of condemnation on the scribes and Pharisees? He said, "Woe unto you scribes, Pharisees, Hypocrites! . . . how shall you escape the damnation of Hell!" Then He said to the common people that the scribes and the Pharisees "sit in Moses' seat," and that they should not imitate their hypocrisy, but they should still obey what they said to do (see Matthew 23:2-3).

The religious leaders were not humbled by the Law. Instead, they were puffed up in their pride, receiving greater condemnation. Jesus was saying, "Let the Law do its work despite the vessels it comes through. Let it bring the knowledge of sin, and prepare your heart for grace."

The Law cannot justify, cleanse, forgive, or even help the sinner. It is merely a mirror so that he might see his true state. It just shows him that he is helplessly dirty. However, the true convert doesn't throw away the mirror after he is cleansed. He lives in respect to the Law. Once he is washed, he wants to stay clean, so he therefore checks the mirror to make sure he lives a Law-abiding life in Christ. He is not bound by the Law in any way, to keep a certain day, etc., but he walks "in the Law of the Lord." He walks in love, and love is the fulfilling of the Law. He doesn't lie to, steal from, or hate his neighbor. If you paid a massive fine for me and saved me from a long prison sentence, and I became lawless again, it is obvious that I haven't seen your sacrificial love in paying my debt to the law.

The Church as a whole has forsaken the Law of God, yet the Ten Commandments should be as intertwined into the Church as the ten curtains were in the tabernacle: "Moreover you shall make the tabernacle with ten curtains woven of fine linen thread, and blue and purple and scarlet yarn; with artistic designs of cherubim you shall weave them" (Exodus 26:1).

The curtains of the Law are upheld in the "fine linen of the righteousness of the saints," the blue and purple of the royal priesthood, and the scarlet of the redeeming blood of the Savior. Separate Law from the gospel, and you expose the Holy Place to a degenerate and corrupt world. To enter without the High Priest will be to the eternal detriment of the professing convert.

6

Ten Candlesticks of Gold

I liked Benson. He was a native Micronesian who was now a full-time missionary. He was one of those powerfully built men who looked like a grizzly bear, but proved to be more cuddly than grizzly. Benson would laugh at almost everything I said.

It was good to see him again. I was the guest speaker at a camp, and I happened to be in the same tent as giggly Benson.

A short time after the light was turned out, Benson went outside the tent. During the night, I saw the shadow of a figure sit up, as though he was about to say something. So, with the usual tongue in cheek humor he seemed to appreciate so much, I said, *"Shut up and go to sleep!"* That normally would have made him chuckle, but instead, he immediately laid down and I never heard another sound from him.

In the morning, I found that it wasn't Benson who slept there, *but another young man I had never seen before.* The first words he heard from the guest speaker were, *"Shut up and go to sleep!"*

I apologized and explained about the misunderstanding. My problem was a presumption I had made in the dark. I presumed I was speaking to Benson, when I wasn't.

The Ten Commandments are like the "ten candlesticks of gold" that were in Solomon's temple (see 2 Chronicles 4:7) to give light to those whose understanding is darkened. *If they cannot see the Holy Place, they will presume that it is not their place to be holy.* If they are left in the dark, like my experience with Benson, they will make a false assumption.

The Commandments are like the ten tables in the temple (see 2 Chronicles 4:8), on which the Bread of Life is placed, so that those who eat may "never hunger." They are analogous to the "instrument of ten strings," upon which David's praises were sweet to the ears of God. He loves His Law, which His Word says is the very "form of knowledge and truth" (Romans 2:20). It was His love for the Law of righteousness, and for sinners, that drove the Savior to the Cross. To teach the Law is to be great in God's Kingdom (see Matthew 5:19).

The unregenerate nature is like the revengeful, murderous, deceitful, and self-promoting Absalom. But when the Commandments come, like the "ten young men" who surrounded Absalom as he hung upon a tree, they strike him to death (see 2 Samuel 18:15). The Law nails the sinner to the tree of Calvary. It slays the sinful nature.

If the Ten Commandments could speak, they would say as the ten men said to Ishmael, "Do not kill us, for we have treasures of wheat, barley, oil, and honey in the field" (Jeremiah 41:8). God's Law can put "treasure in earthen vessels" into the field of the world. It can produce wheat and not tares. The Law of God can bring us to the oil of the Holy Spirit and the sweet honey of the gospel of Salvation.

The Commandments are like the dark shadow that moved ten degrees and convinced Hezekiah that the good news he heard was from God. They may look like a pile of sun-bleached bones of a dead prophet from the ancient past, lying in a cave's shadow. But throw the sinner onto those dry bones, and he will spring to life again through the power of the gospel.

The function of the Law is not merely to kill, but to bring the "dead in trespasses" sinner to the resurrection life that is in Jesus Christ. It brings him from the "Law of sin and death" into the "law of life in Christ Jesus."

The Commandments are like the ten women who baked bread which could not satisfy (see Leviticus 26:26). The Law leaves the human heart with a hunger which only the Bread of Life can fulfill. The ten oracles of the Law are like the ten men who witnessed the redemption of Ruth by Boaz (see Ruth 4:2). The Commandments stand as an indictment against the sinner until he is safely in the arms of the Redeemer.

The Body of Christ yielded to the devil's temptings to turn the solid stones of the Law into soft palatable bread. Instead of using the hard threatenings of the Commandments to drive sinners to the Savior, they have been sliced, buttered, and presented to the world as a savory morsel of morality, something for which they were never intended.

Ten Candlesticks of Gold

Ten Kneeling Camels

In Genesis, chapter 24, we find the story of Abraham, sending his servant to find a bride for his only begotten son, Isaac. The servant took ten camels and traveled to Mesopotamia to the city of Nahor. When he arrived at the city, he caused his ten camels to kneel down outside the city before the "well of water at evening time, the time when women go out to draw water." Abraham's servant knew the identity of the bride-to-be because:

1. She was a virgin (vs. 16).
2. She had consideration for the ten camels (vs. 19), in fact, she *ran* back to the well to get more water for the camels.

The bride-to-be totally accepted that this incident was the hand of God, and willingly gave consent to marriage.

When they called Rebekah and asked her if she would go with him, she said, "I will go." When she saw her husband-to-be, she dismounted from her camel and covered herself with a veil, then she became his wife, and he loved her (see Genesis 24:64-67).

Bride of Heaven, Pride of Hell

God the Father sent the servant of His Holy Spirit to search out a Bride for His only begotten Son. He has chosen to use the ten camels of the Ten Commandments to carry this special message from His Lord. Those who work with the Holy Spirit will know that it is His way to make the ten camels of the Law kneel before the Well of Salvation. The Ten Commandments line up perfectly before the living water of the gospel of Jesus Christ, the One from whom all who thirst may drink.

While we may not be able to clearly distinguish the Bride of Christ from the rest of the world, the Holy Spirit knows that:

> 1. She is a virgin. She is not a harlot who has defiled herself with mankind.
> 2. The primary reason she draws water from the Well of Salvation, is to satisfy the ten thirsting camels of a holy and just Law.

She has respect, honor, and esteem for the Commandments of God. She is not a worker of lawlessness. Like Paul, she says, "I delight in the

Law of God" (Romans 7:22). In fact, the virgin of the Bride of Christ declares, "I will *run* the way of your Commandments" (Psalm 119:32). Why? Because the Law is perfect, holy, just, and good, and the God-given means to convert the soul to everlasting life in Jesus Christ.

The Servant doesn't have to twist her arm with psychological manipulation to get a decision to follow her prospective husband. She comes *willingly.* In Genesis 24:22, we see that the servant gave the virgin "a golden earring of half a shekel weight, and two bracelets for her hands of ten shekels weight of gold."

The true convert has been given an ear for the gospel, the golden ear of understanding. The reason she understands the good news is because the two bracelets, like golden handcuffs, have made sure that she was "kept under the Law, shut up unto the faith which should afterwards be revealed" (Galatians 3:23).

She then forsakes all she has to travel across the barren desert of this life and looks forward with unspeakable anticipation to the time she will see her Husband face to face. She is always ready, keeping herself unspotted from the world, making sure that her lamp is trimmed, that she is covered with the mantle of righteousness, and will fall prostrate at His Holy feet when she sees Him as He is.

7

A Place Without Hope

We tend to despise the ten half-brothers of Joseph when they stripped him of his tunic and cast him into a pit to die, but God had His purposes. Who knows what happened in the darkness of that hole? The Bible tells us that it was a place without hope: "and the pit was empty, there was no water in it" (Genesis 37:24).

Perhaps it was then that Joseph truly cried out to God. Perhaps it was the beginning of the making of such strength of character that could be so God-fearing and so forgiving. God delivered him in His time.

In the same way, we shouldn't despise the Ten Commandments when they strip the sinner of his self-righteousness and cast him into the pit of despair. Who knows what is happening in the darkness of his heart? There certainly is no hope in the Law. It is empty, with not a drop of the water of life in it. Perhaps it is then, while in such a hopeless state, that he will call out to God and ask Him to purge him with hyssop, and wash him whiter than snow. It is then in the blackness, like the Philippian jailer, he calls for light. The earthquake of the Law can make a man change his priorities, and therefore its office should never be despised. It is God's way to cast down before He builds up, to humble before He exalts, to kill before He makes alive, to have a man tremble because he has sinned, before He comforts him with mercy. God "revives the spirit of the humble." The Law turns the stomach sour, but makes the gospel sweet in the mouth.

When the king of Syria sent Naaman the leper to the king of Israel seeking healing, he also sent "ten talents of silver and ten changes of clothing" as a gift. Ironically, the king of Israel would need some new clothes. When he read the letter, he tore his own clothes in frustration (see 2 Kings 5:5-8).

The letter of the Law kills. It *cannot* heal the leprosy of sin. It makes a man rend his heart, not his garments. The letter brings the leprous sinner to the door of Him who can make him clean from his plague.

When fiery serpents were sent among Israel, it caused them to admit they had sinned, and drove them to Moses to be saved (see Numbers 21:6-7). The serpents carried a deadly bite. Jesus specifically cited this passage in reference to salvation from sin, in John 3:14. The Ten Commandments are like ten biting serpents that carry with them the venomous curse of the Law. It drives sinners to Him who is lifted up, to Him who has redeemed us from the "curse of the Law, being made a curse for us."

Someone once said, "Sin is as great as He who is offended by it." God is unspeakably offended by sin, but rich in mercy, and ready to comfort all who call upon Him. Therefore, if a Philippian jailer falls at your feet in contrition and cries, *"What must I do to be saved?"* then give him grace as you would water to a dying man.

But if a man curses God, mocks sin and despises the name of the Savior, leave him in the desert and let the heat of the Law burn his flesh until he cries, "Give me water, lest I die!" Pray for that day to come soon, and ask that God uses your hand to give him the water of life when he is ready.

Priming the Ear of Lazarus

Jesus was in no hurry to raise Lazarus from the grave, and he who trusts God in salvation will not frustrate a work of grace. Those however, who don't see the need of the Holy Spirit to convict of sin, righteousness, and judgment, may play music outside the tomb of the sinner. They may have counselors carry the corpse out of the sepulcher, and they may even prop the corpse up under his arms, but "Lazarus" is four days dead in his sins (see Ephesians 2:5). The stench of the filthy rags of his righteous deeds reaches high Heaven.

The Church *cannot* bring life to his corrupted flesh without the help of the Holy Spirit. The function of the Law is to prime the ear of Lazarus to hear the voice of the Son of God.

Salvation is a work of grace. Even the preaching of the Law, if not quickened by the Spirit, is nothing but dead letter, unable to bring a glimmer of light to a soul. Man can do nothing to save himself. Neither can a man do a thing to save another unless God works in and through him. This is not Calvinism. It is simple Bible theology.

I was once waiting to preach when I stepped out of a church building for some fresh air. The second I stepped through the door, a tire on a parked car directly in front of me suddenly burst. The owners of the vehicle knew that there was a nail in the tire, but rather than change it, they risked the drive to church.

When the nail of the Law penetrates the heart of the sinner, it may be a matter of time before we see visible results. But when a preacher of the gospel steps onto the scene, he will be but a spectator in a true work of grace. A sinner who has previously been nailed by the Law will eventually get the point of the gospel, *once he comes under the pressure of Holy Spirit conviction.*

David's Ten Women

The Church, in setting aside the Ten Commandments is like David when he "took the ten women, his concubines" (2 Samuel 20:3), and would have nothing to do with them because they were defiled in his eyes. Yet they had merely suffered as a result of his own sin. They could have borne him many children, but instead remained barren.

True, there are many who have used the Law unlawfully and defiled it in the sight of godly men. The hammer of the Law is only good if it is used to fasten sinners to the Cross. If it is wielded unlawfully in legalism or in seeking justification, the blame lies in the hand using the hammer, and not in the tool itself (see 1 Timothy 1:8).

If we make the distinction between the *legitimate* and the *unlawful* use of the Law, we can then enjoy the benefits of the Ten Commandments. We can see children born into the Kingdom as the Law opens the hearts of sinners to the seed of the gospel.

As with Moses, God has placed in the hands of the Church the authority to call down the ten plagues of the Ten Commandments to awaken the world to His awesome power. Why was it that so many did the seemingly foolish act of placing blood on their door posts? It was because they had seen the fearful plagues which came upon Egypt. They knew that this was a God who was to be feared, the God who commanded thunder and lightning to flash and roar across the heavens. This was the very purpose of the plagues (see Exodus 9:14).

The design of the Ten Commandments is not to torment the world, but to put the fear of God in people's hearts, so that "they may know that there is none like the Lord," and so they might apply the blood of the Savior to the door posts of their lives. The Law shows the sinner sin in its true light. The Commandment turns the river of sin's pleasure into undrinkable blood. Once he is aware that God requires an account, he can no longer enjoy the delights of his transgressions in ignorant and reckless abandonment. It shows him that his warm and darling sins are nothing but filthy flies, devouring locusts, and hideous, cold-blooded frogs. The licentious bed of adultery is no longer pleasant license for lasciviousness when filled with loathsome lice. The Law hails down the wrath of God. It plagues him with the fire of a tormented conscience. The Ten Commandments afflict him with boils so painful that he can no longer "sit in the seat of the scornful." It surrounds him with the thick darkness of the shadow of death, until he calls for the light of the glorious gospel of Christ who is the image of God. The plagues are not pleasant, but utterly needful, or there will be no applying of the blood in faith.

The Law of God troubles the pool of iniquity in the heart of a man. It leaves him in a hopeless state. It prepares him for the One who says, "Will you be made whole?"

The Big One

We are told that if you are in your house and there is an earthquake, the safest place is under the door posts. It is the door posts that are often left standing when all else collapses. We are also told that the safest thing to do if your house is filled with smoke, is to drop to your knees and inhale life-giving oxygen, which is trapped close to the floor.

When Isaiah saw a vision of the Lord, "the posts of the door moved at the voice of him that cried, and the house was filled with smoke" (Isaiah 6:4). In other words, he was in *immediate and terrible danger of being crushed to death*. His house was also filled with smoke. He therefore, without delay carried out the life-saving procedure. He dropped to his knees, and was able to continue breathing through life-giving repentance (vs. 5).

The holiness of the Law does for the sinner that which Isaiah's vision did for him. It takes him, by vision, into the presence of God. It moves the posts of his door. It shows him his immediate and terrible danger of being ground to powder. It shakes him out of his complacency. Like the Philippian jailer, it makes him feel the earthquake of God's wrath. The fiery Law fills his "house" with a choking smoke, and lets him smell the blaze of Almighty God's indignation. *It alarms him*. He will perish without repentance. He *must* run from his house of sin. It makes him cry, "Woe is me! For I am undone. What must I do to be saved?"

It also produces in him that which was produced in Isaiah after such a terrifying experience. It puts fire in his lips (vss. 6-7). He knows the terror of the Lord, so he persuades men. He cannot but speak that which he has seen and heard. Gratitude for such mercy provokes him to say, "Here I am; send me" (vs. 8).

In doing so, the Law shows itself to be just and good. Sin is a tantalizing bait on Hell's hidden hook. The Law takes him by the neck and constrains him to look closely at that on which he is nibbling.

The Ten Commandments are like the ten proclamations given to Nehemiah, warning him of the power of his enemies (see Nehemiah 4:12).

In *Pilgrim's Progress*, Christian said, "It was he (the Law) who did bind my heavy burden upon me." Faithful agrees: "Aye. Had it not been for him, we had both of us stayed in the City of Destruction."

"Then he did to us a favor," answered Christian. Faithful then shows how the Law alarms us: "Aye. Albeit, he did it none too gently." Then Christian says, "Well, at least he played the part of a schoolmaster and showed us our need. It was he who drove us to the Cross."

The Law turns from being an enemy of the sinner into an ally--to those who find themselves driven to the foot of the Cross. The Ten Commandments become true friends to the feeble sinner. They rip off the covering of his self-righteousness, and break it up. They gently lower him down on his bed of infirmity . . . to the feet of Him who can say, "Son, your sins are forgiven" (Mark 2:3-5).

There were ten lepers whose terrible disease compelled them to stand afar off and cry to Jesus for mercy (see Luke 17:12), and there are Ten Commandments, who, as priests of the Law, diagnose the terrible disease of sin. They compel the leprous sinner who stands afar off, to *call* upon Jesus for mercy.

The Law brings us to the feet of Jesus where we wash His feet with our tears of repentance.

8

Don't Leave Me

I was in Baltimore without a meeting on a Sunday night, so I decided to change my air ticket to go home early.

As usual, the phone operator gave the name of the airline. Then she said that her name was Fran, asking how she could be of help to me. I explained my situation, and made her laugh a little to a point where I had the liberty to ask about her spiritual life. I said, "Fran, are you a Christian?" She said, "No. I don't accept the virgin birth." I explained to her that wasn't the issue with her at the moment, and that her big problem was the Ten Commandments. I asked, "Have you ever told a lie?" She said she had. She also admitted that she had stolen. When I explained that Jesus said that lust was the same as adultery in God's sight, and asked her if she had lusted, she said. "Of course."

Gently, I said, "Fran, by your own admission, you are a lying, thieving, adulterer at heart. You have to face God on Judgment Day, *and we have only looked at three of the Ten Commandments*." I then said, "I would like a window seat if possible." She didn't appreciate the subject change, and said, *"Don't leave me like this!"* Gently, I said, "What's wrong Fran, don't you like being left with your conscience?" I further went on to reason with her about her salvation, about Judgment Day, then the Cross.

We shouldn't be afraid to make the sinner tremble. Men like Whitefield and others preached until the Law "stopped the mouth," and men hung their heads in shame. A parent looks for that in a child who has been disobedient. A resurrected conscience is the first sign of the beginnings of the work of the Holy Spirit.

Fran didn't get mad at me. I wasn't judging her. *She* was the one who admitted her sins. Besides, what could she say--"I thought lying, theft, etc. were right?" It is because of the ally of conscience that we can say "hard" things (in love) to sinners.

It is interesting to note that the conscience

doesn't join in with the pleasures of sin. The unregenerate person loves sin with all of his heart, mind, soul, and strength. However, the conscience, the judge in the courtroom of the mind, stands aloof and makes an impartial judgment. It is the "work of the Law". written on our hearts, the "conscience bearing witness, and their thoughts the mean while accusing or else excusing one another" (Romans 2:15, KJV). The judge gives a *guilty* or *not guilty* judgment of that which is evidenced before it.

In parts of Africa, during the drought season, antelope are drawn by thirst to pools of muddy water. Without drink they will die of thirst. Hidden in the foul waters lie hungry and vicious crocodiles. The only thing visible in the water to the discerning, is the naked eye of the monster as it watches every movement of the antelope.

Desire so consumes the animal it slowly ventures to the water's edge, and completely lets down its God-given guard as it drinks in the life-giving liquid. Suddenly, great jaws open and, amidst the splashing of water, the animal is pulled to a terrible death.

The sinner is drawn to the muddy pool of iniquity by his uncontrollable thirst for sin. The cries of his God-given conscience are muffled at the sight of what lies before him. Without sin, he feels he will die. Suddenly, death seizes upon him in an instant and he is gone forever, swallowed by the jaws of everlasting Hell.

The Law reveals the crocodile *before* it attacks. As he drinks in the waters of sin, he suddenly sees sin's terrible form as it lies hidden in the pool. This is what Paul is speaking about in Romans 7:8-12. The Law showed him the appetite in the eye of the beast, causing him to draw back from the foul pool of iniquity.

So Long Pal!

We get regular calls on our 800 number from dyslexic men, who mistakenly transpose the last two digits of the number they are calling. Very early one morning a deep-voiced gentleman phoned, thinking he was calling a farm supplies firm. I told him that he had transposed the last two numbers, then said to make sure that he read his Bible. He said he wouldn't, because he was an atheist. For the next few minutes I reasoned with him about the necessity of having a maker for everything that was made. It was a spirited sword fight, but it was merely sword-play. The moment would come when I would have to get my point across, to go for the kill. I took the

Commandments in hand and lunged towards the heart: "Do you think you have kept the Ten Commandments?" He said he thought he had. "Have you ever told a lie?" He had, but would not hold still for a second and admit that he was a liar. He jumped back and forth, insisting that someone who told lies was "human," or told "fibs" or was "weak, like everyone else."

When I pressed the point, he suddenly spat out, "O.K. I'm a liar!" We touched on two other Commandments which he admitted to transgressing, the existence of his conscience, and fact of Judgment Day. Suddenly, his references to evolution, other people's sins, and hypocrisy in the Church were no longer the issue. He was mortally wounded. He staggered backwards and protested, "*I'm a good person!*" I thrust back, "No you're not. You're a lying thief!" The pain was too much for him. He said, "*So long pal!*" and hung up in my ear.

I sat by the phone and thought, *I wish he had stayed in the fight for another minute. I would have told him that he was just adding self-righteousness to his sin. I would also have liked to have told him to study Matthew 24 and Luke 21, and they would prove to him that the Bible is the Word of the Creator.* Then I prayed that God's hand would be upon the man.

About ten seconds later, the phone rang again. When I picked it up, I heard a deep-voiced and mystified man mumble, "What's going on! How did I get *you* again? I tried to call this number, and instead I get one that makes my blood hot."

Hot blood means that life is present. He was no longer a cold-blooded atheist. *I was beside myself with joy.* I told him to read Matthew 24 and Luke 21. Then I told him my name and said he could call our 800 number any time. When he kept mumbling, "Why did I call you again?" I could only think of two alternatives. It was either because he was a dummy, and had called the wrong number again, or that God's hand was upon him. I told him it was because God's hand was upon him. He didn't argue about that, and this time our parting was more congenial.

9

Why the Glory?

May the Church take a look at her state compared to what she should be, and realize that there is a "breach in the house of the Lord." Perhaps then, like Hilkiah the high priest, it will uncover the Book of the Law in the House of the Lord, and use it lawfully. The Law caused King Josiah to tear his clothes in contrition, and God gave him grace, *because he took notice of the Law* (see 2 Kings 22:11,13,19).

When the Law is allowed to do its work, it takes out the hard stones from the ground, leaving soft and tender soil. It humbles and produces contrition. It is like the sun, which rises with a burning heat and causes the sinner's self-righteousness to wither as the grass.

I'm sure you have heard much teaching about

the time the glory of God was so great that the priests of the Lord could not even minister (see 1 Kings 8:10-11). Have you ever wondered why God so manifested Himself in such glory? It happened when Solomon brought the ark of the Lord into the temple. Was it the ark which caused such a wonderful thing to happen? I don't think so. It was because the ark contained the Law (see 1 Kings 8:9). David didn't say, "Oh how I love your *ark*, it is my meditation night and day," neither does Scripture say, "The *ark* of the Lord is perfect, converting the soul." Nor did Paul say, "I delight in the *ark* of God." The fact is, God so esteems His Law, He could not withhold His glorious presence from the temple.

Let the Church . . . the temple of the Holy Spirit . . . give God's Law its due place. May we "magnify the Law and make it honorable" (Isaiah 42:21). The word "honorable" is *adar,* and means "glorious." It may be that we will see such power and glory within the Church, that we will not be able to minister.

A similar thing happened when the priests put their feet in the Jordan (see Joshua 3:1-17). God did a miracle and opened up the river. Was there something special about the priest's feet? No, *they carried the ark which contained the Law.*

Do you think God would have done a miracle

if the priests had deemed the ark too heavy with the stone tablets inside, and tipped the Law onto the dirt? I don't think so, yet that is what the modern Church does with the Law of God. There are many who love God, yet, in their ignorance, they despise the Law.

It was J.C. Ryle who said of the Law, "But never, never let us despise it. It is the symptom of an ignorant ministry, and unhealthy state of religion, when the Law is reckoned unimportant. The true Christian delights in God's Law (Romans 7:22)."

When God personally speaks to you about the right use of the Commandments, like Moses, your face will shine as you come down from the holy mountain. But, also like Moses, you will feel a sense of frustration and anger as you see the Law being broken within the Church, as well as in the world. Throw the tablets of the Law down at their feet. It will put the fear of God in the hearts of those who dance around the golden calf of immorality. Show them how they have broken the Law into a thousand pieces.

Think of Jonah, who, like Adam, ran from the presence of the Lord. God sent a great storm, but Jonah lay asleep in the lower parts of the ship. It was the captain that awoke him and told him to call upon his God, that he might not perish.

The sinner is fleeing from the presence of the Lord. There is a great storm of God's wrath gathering over him. But sin, the very cause of the storm, lies asleep deep in his heart. It takes the Law of God, in the hand of the Captain of our salvation, to awaken him to call upon his God that he might not perish.

After Jonah's dark experience with the great fish, an entire city repented and turned to the Lord. How was Nineveh awakened to such a sweeping repentance? They understood the message preached--that God was threatening to be violent, that He was angry, and that they were about to perish (see Jonah 3:8-9).

Snake in the Pews

The presence of the Ark of the Covenant was synonymous to victory. After Uzzah was killed for touching the ark, David left it in the house of Obededom, and his house was blessed because of its presence (see 2 Samuel 6:11). When it was taken from Israel by the Philistines, it was said that the glory departed "for the ark of God is taken" (1 Samuel 4:22).

When it was placed in front of a Philistine demon god, it had the effect of destroying the idol (see 1 Samuel 5:3-4).

Why the Glory?

When the Law of Moses is put back into the ark of the gospel, it will rid the land of idolatry and be to the downfall of the enemy, wherever it is taken. That's why Satan so hates it.

I was getting ready to minister in Singapore in 1988, when just before I was about to teach on the Law, they found a snake in the pews. Someone held its body still while another person stomped on its head.

That's what we must do through prayer to Satan, so that this teaching can have free course in the Church.

I often talk to Christians who recognize the imperative nature of preaching the Law before grace, but they are deeply frustrated because they are surrounded by others who carry on evangelizing with modern methods. Their methods are, in truth, counterproductive to the cause of the gospel. They are so sure that they are doing God's will, they won't listen to something that mentions the Law--that hints of what they consider to be "legalism." These Christians are like the man who was brought to Jesus who was deaf and had an impediment in his speech. He had never heard his own faulty speech. He had to be brought to Jesus to be healed.

We must do what Jesus did. He looked towards

heaven and sighed (see Mark 7:34). It is fervent, heart-felt prayer that opens ears. When the man's ears were opened, then he spoke plainly. The same will happen with the Church, if we pray earnestly that God will open her ears to this teaching.

In May of 1996, I was staying with a couple named Steve and Beckie, just outside of Reno, Nevada. On the way back from having lunch at the local pastor's house, we ran over a snake on the road. At my insistence, we turned the car around and drove back to look at it. It looked like a rattlesnake. It was about five feet long, and was still moving. As I studied it from a distance, I could see that its neck had been broken. I quickly grabbed a stick, courageously put it into Steve's hand, pushed him towards the snake and said, "Go get it!" Then, with my encouragement, he picked it up and flicked it off the road.

Satan's neck was broken at the Cross. God has placed the stick of His Law into our hands, and commanded us to "Go." It is the Law of God that will get the devil out of the road, so that sinners might freely come to Christ.

In the late 70's, a man named Herb Frick and a few of his fickled friends saw what they thought was a dead rattlesnake on the road. They stopped their pickup truck, picked up the snake, put it on the dashboard, and drove off with their "trophy."

They said that some time later it seemed that someone pushed the snake's "life-button," and it sat up as though it was about to strike. Every one of those young men bailed out of that vehicle like greased lightning.

The sinner doesn't know what danger he puts himself in when he trifles with sin. As far as he is concerned it can't harm him. He boasts of his sinful exploits. They are his trophy. The Law pushes sin's life-button . . . "For without the Law, sin was dead" (Romans 7:8). It makes it sit up to strike him. It puts the fear of God in his heart and compels him bail out of the vehicle of iniquity.

Things Old and New

It was an *ark* made of bulrushes which contained the child Moses, the deliverer of Israel, and it is the golden ark of the gospel which should embody the Law of Moses. Moses should precede Jesus: "If they hear not Moses . . . neither will they be persuaded, though one rose from the dead" (Luke 16:31).

The first attempt to bring the ark into Jerusalem was a disaster because all things were not done "according to the pattern." Their song and dance turned sour when God revealed His wrath at their failure to carry it as they should. However, on the second attempt the difference was that the "Levites" carried the ark. They wore "fine linen," and so did the King (see 1 Chronicles 15:27). When the Church understands the purpose of the Law, she will make sure she is wearing "the fine linen of the righteousness of the saints" (Revelation 19:8), and then we will have much to sing and dance about--we will see true revival. If you take the time to study authentic revivals, you will see that a new respect for the Law of God preceded a genuine move of God.

We should be like the scribe Jesus spoke of who was instructed "unto the Kingdom of Heaven." He said that the scribe was like a "householder who brings forth out of his treasure things old and new" (Matthew 13:52).

We are of the "household of God" (Ephesians 2:19). If we are suitably instructed unto the Kingdom of Heaven, we will preach the whole counsel of God, made up of the Law of God and the grace that is in Jesus Christ--things old and things new.

10

Bait For the Hooker

Satan's greatest triumph has been to keep the use of the Law of God away from the eyes of the Church. The result has been masses of lawless "converts." These are people who seem to love Jesus Christ, but a closer examination will show the discerning Christian that something is radically wrong.

In Proverbs, chapter 7, the Scriptures open with strong admonitions regarding the Law of God. The Bible tells us to esteem the Law, to treasure it and keep it as "the apple of your eye." We are told to bind the Law on the fingers (one Commandment for each digit), and to write it on the tables of our heart. This is the way to gain wisdom and understanding, because the function of the Law is to act as a schoolmaster to bring to us knowledge and understanding. The Bible says of the Messiah, "By His knowledge My righteous Servant shall justify many" (Isaiah 53:11). The ministry of Jesus was to give knowledge of salvation to humanity: "And we know that the Son of God has come and has given us an understanding" (1 John 5:20). He was to "magnify (promote) the Law and make it honorable," and that's what He did with the Law in the Sermon on the Mount.

The end result of the Law, or the "Commandment," should be that it produces in the convert "love from a pure heart, from a good conscience, and from sincere faith" (1 Timothy 1:5). The effect of the fruit of the Law, is that it will keep us from the "immoral woman" (Proverbs 7:5).

The Mantle of the Harlot

Let's now look closely at the "immoral woman," the harlot of Proverbs, chapter 7:

For at the window of my house I looked through my lattice, and saw among the simple, I perceived among the youths, a young man devoid of understanding, passing along the street near her corner, and he took the path to her house. In the twilight, in the evening, in the black and dark night. And there a woman met him, with the attire of a harlot, and a crafty heart. She was loud and rebellious, her feet would not stay at home. At times she was outside, at times in the open square, lurking at every corner. So she caught him and kissed him; with an impudent face she said to him: *"I have peace offerings with me; today I have paid my vows. So I came out to meet you, diligently to seek your face, and I have found you. I have spread my bed with tapestry, colored coverings of Egyptian linen. I have perfumed my bed with myrrh, aloes, and cinnamon. Come, let us take our fill with love until morning; let us delight ourselves with love, for my husband is not home; he has gone on a long journey; he has taken a bag of money with him, and will come home on the appointed day."*

With her enticing speech she caused him to yield, with her flattering lips she seduced him. Immediately he went after her, as an ox goes to the slaughter, or as a fool to the correction of the stocks, till an arrow struck his liver. As a bird hastens to the snare, he did not know it would cost him his life.

Now therefore, listen to me, my children; pay attention to the words of my mouth: do not let your heart turn aside to her ways, do not stray into her paths; for she has cast down many wounded, and all who were slain by her were strong men. Her house is the way to Hell, descending to the dark chambers of death (Proverbs 7:6-27).

Let's summarize what happened:

1. The youth was without *understanding* (vs. 7).
2. The harlot was *crafty, loud and rebellious* (vs. 11).
3. She had *peace offerings* and had paid vows (vs. 14).
4. Her bed was decked with *Egyptian* linen (vs. 16).
5. She *perfumed* her bed (vs. 17).
6. She flattered and *seduced* the youth (vs. 21).
7. He *immediately* followed her (vs. 22).

First, the youth is without understanding. Here we have a vivid picture of the work of a harlot. The Scriptures say a youth who was lacking in understanding roamed the streets. This is a depiction of the unregenerate, whose understanding is darkened, being alienated from the life of God through the ignorance that is in him (see Ephesians 4:18). He is wandering the streets of futility. This youth is a potential customer, *because of his ignorance.*

Second, she was crafty, loud, and rebellious. The Bible tells us, "The mouth of an immoral woman is like a deep pit." She drinks in iniquity like water. This loud, rebellious, and crafty harlot catches the youth in the blackness of the night and begins to seduce him (vss. 9-14). Here is the difference between the true and the false church. The Harlot church (the word "harlot" is capitalized to signify the Harlot church and differentiate it from the harlot of Proverbs 7), doesn't have the ornament of a meek and quiet spirit. She lacks the gentleness of the wisdom which is from above, the brokenness of a contrite spirit. The false church is concerned with growth, numbers, power, and possessions rather than with the fact that souls must repent or they will perish. Close examination will show that her desire is for pleasure and for riches. Her wisdom is earthly, sensual, devilish. She preaches that gain is godliness, and her god is mammon. She manifests the works of the flesh rather than the fruit of the Spirit. She will pass by the bleeding stranger on the road to Jericho on the pretense of doing the will of God. She will go through his pockets rather than heal his wounds.

Third, she had "peace offerings," and had paid her vows. The whore says to the youth, "I have peace offerings . . . I have paid my vows" (vs. 14). In other words she assures him that he can sin and still find forgiveness with God. That's the promise of the Harlot church. She allows the grace of our God to be used as an occasion of the flesh.

The peace offering is first mentioned directly after the giving of the Law to Moses (see Exodus 20:24). According to *Unger's Bible Dictionary*: "The peace offerings have their root in the state of grace, with its fellowship with God, and find their culminating point in the sacrificial feast. They served to establish the Hebrew more firmly in the fellowship of the Divine grace; to be mindful of God when in possession and enjoyment of the Divine mercies" (*Peace Offerings, p. 948*).

Fourth, her bed was covered with "Egyptian" linen. The Harlot church has an appearance of righteousness, but it is only skin deep because her bed is covered with the covering of "Egyptian linen" (vs. 16) rather than the "fine linen which is the righteousness of the saints." Her standards are the standards of Egypt . . . the world . . . not the standards of the Kingdom of God. She says you *can* be a friend of the world and a friend of God; you *can* serve God and mammon. Hers is the ear-tickling gospel of compromise.

Don't be fooled by her outward appearance. She is like sinful Tyrus, with a mantle of "fine linen with broidered work from Egypt . . . blue and purple" (Ezekiel 27:7), but God sees her heart, and will bring His great wrath upon her as He did on Tyrus.

In contrast, the Chaste Virgin, like Joseph, is given "fine linen" as a covering (see Genesis 41:42). The Holy Spirit carefully takes the Body of Christ and wraps it in "fine linen" for a covering (see Mark 15:46), as Joseph of Arimathea did with the body of Christ. She is not loud and boisterous like the Harlot, but her beauty is of "the hidden person of the heart, with the incorruptible ornament of a gentle and quiet spirit, which is very precious in the sight of God." She does nothing "through strife or vainglory, but in lowliness of mind" she esteems others better than herself. Her godly priorities are seen in the actions of Job when he was stripped of all his wealth and family. He tore his mantle, fell to the ground and worshipped God (see Job 1:20). She would give up her mantle . . . the righteousness that brings life . . . to honor Him to whom she is espoused. The Chaste Virgin so loves Him that shed His blood for her, that she "hates" her own life in comparison (see Luke 14:26).

She says, "Let him kiss me with the kisses of his mouth: for your love is better than wine. Because of the savor of your good ointments, your name is as ointment poured forth, therefore do the virgins love you" (Song of Solomon 1:2-3). She knows that what God has joined together, man cannot separate. She is secure in His love. She is fully persuaded that neither death, nor life, nor angels, nor principalities, nor powers, nor things present, nor things to come, nor height, nor depth, nor any other creature, shall be able to separate her from the love of God, which is in Christ Jesus her Lord.

She is careful to guard what she looks at and what she listens to. It must be true, honest, and just. She makes sure that it is pure, lovely, of good report, and if there is any virtue, she thinks on these things. She also makes sure that the words of her mouth and the meditations of her heart are acceptable in God's sight. If her eye offends her, she would rather pluck it out and cast it from her than have her whole body cast into Hell. She exercises herself to always have a conscience void of offense towards God and man. She cultivates the fear of God because she knows that her God is a consuming fire. She has been called to glory and virtue and is a partaker of the Divine Nature, having escaped the corruption that is in the world through lust. Therefore she gives all diligence, and adds to her faith, virtue, and to virtue knowledge, and because of these qualities, she is neither barren nor unfruitful in the knowledge of our Lord Jesus Christ (see 2 Peter 1:3-8).

The heart of the Harlot church is not after God. Like King Saul, she is a rebel. To her the sacrifice of praise is better than obedience. She worships, but she doesn't serve. Saul, in his usual unstable manner, reached out and tore the mantle of the prophet. So this double-minded and unstable Harlot is a tool of the devil to tear at the mantle of the Church. Through murmuring, complaining, back-biting, and gossip, she lends her sharp and whispering tongue to the devil, and separates the chief of friends. She doesn't strive "for the faith of the gospel," but endeavors only to further her own lustful desires.

The Chaste Virgin is a servant; the Harlot wants to be served. The Virgin seeks to give; the Harlot, only to get.

Fifth, she perfumed her bed. The harlot wanted the youth to enter her bed which she had perfumed with myrrh, aloe, and cinnamon. She had the knowledge of that which is sacred, and had the gall to use an adulteration of the holy anointing oil to perfume the bed of her harlotry (see Exodus 30:23). So the Harlot church has the effrontery to adulterate the anointing of the Holy Spirit with the things of the world. This is why she has an attraction to the carnal mind of man. Like the sweet perfume of a prostitute, the aroma of the modern gospel seduces his natural senses, promising the pleasures of peace, joy, love, and happiness.

Sixth, she seduced the youth. The Hebrew whore whispered, "Let us delight ourselves with love," when in truth she doesn't know the meaning of the word. The false church speaks much of the love of God, but her failure to show concern enough to warn sinners to flee from the wrath to come reveals that she is a stranger to true biblical love.

When Israel wandered from God, He said they were like an adulterous harlot (see Jeremiah 3:1). This thought continues in the New Testament. James, after speaking of those who are lawless, says that the reason God doesn't answer their prayers is because they are filled with their own ways. Then he calls them "adulterers and adulteresses." The God of the New Testament hasn't changed. He is jealous, and will have no other gods before Him.

Then James puts his finger on the problem. In addressing those who claim to be Christians and yet fight amongst themselves, he abruptly says *"Cleanse your hands, you sinners"* (James 4:8). Their problem was that they named the name of Jesus, but never repented. They laughed when they should have mourned, they had joy, when they should have had heaviness. They never knew what it was to labor and be heavy-laden under the weight of their sins, because they didn't realize their state before a holy God. Then in verse 11, James uses the Law as his point of moral reference . . . as he does a number of times in the epistle . . . to bring the knowledge of sin.

To the adulterous Harlot church the Law is totally irrelevant. She has no knowledge of sin: "Such is the way of an adulterous woman; she

111

eats, and wipes her mouth, and says, 'I have done no wickedness'" (Proverbs 30:20). All that matters to her is pleasure, power, pomp, performance, prosperity, prominence, popularity, prestige, size, and success. She is built on lawlessness, and from there she promotes lawlessness, all in the name of Christ. The gospel is fostered as nothing more than a means of life enrichment.

Seventh, he immediately follows her. The harlot of Proverbs, chapter 7, says that her husband has gone on a long journey, that he would come home "on the appointed day." She wants the youth to feel confident that there is no danger of her husband returning and discovering their sin.

The false convert is deceived into *cleaving* to the Harlot church and becoming "one flesh" with her. He says that he is Christ's, but he doesn't see the peril of compromise. He doesn't understand the depth of the apostle Paul's warning: "Do you not know that your bodies are members of Christ? Shall I take members of Christ and make them members of a harlot? Certainly not! Or do you not know that he that is joined to a harlot is one body with her. For 'The two,' He says, 'shall be one flesh'" (1 Corinthians 6:15-16).

He begins to "drink with the drunken" and say

"My lord delays his coming" (Matthew 24:48). The Husband is on a long journey. He *compromises* his Christianity--"com" meaning, "together." He *promises* his allegiance to the Savior "together" with the world. His vow to the Savior is a falsehood. He is like Demas, who hid among the brethren, but in his heart he was tailgating the world. He has a double life, and is like the drunk who walked into a room, saw two candles and blew one out. He was seeing double, and blew out his only light.

Jesus told His disciples to be "shod with sandals; and not put on two coats" (Mark 6:9). The false convert does neither. His feet are not shod with the gospel of Peace, and he *does* put on two coats. He wears one for the Kingdom of God and one for the world.

The harlot is a deep pit and a narrow well. She "lies in wait for a victim, and increases the unfaithful among men" (Proverbs 23:27-28). The spurious convert falls into the narrow well of hypocrisy. Without the enabling grace of God, he is powerless to get out. He becomes enclosed in the gross darkness of self-deception.

The harlot is not only sinful, she is unfaithful to her vows. She is a *married* harlot. She is as "rottenness to the bones" of her husband. She has been espoused to another and yet she indulges in the pleasures of illicit sex. She cannot claim she did it merely for the money, because it is obvious from what she says that her husband has provided for her.

The false convert is a hypocrite and is more guilty than someone who sins in ignorance. He knows of the sayings of Jesus, and therefore no longer has a cloak for his sin. He is an "unstable" soul, having "eyes full of adultery, and that cannot cease from sin."

The Church, in contrast, is without guile. Her vow is binding. She is a servant of her Lord. She is an espoused, spotless virgin, separate from the world, promised only to her Husband, the High Priest of our faith, Jesus Christ: "He that is the high priest among his brethren . . . he shall take a wife in her virginity . . . an harlot . . . shall he not take: but he shall take a virgin of his own people to wife" (Leviticus 21:10-14).

The High Priest of our profession is coming for a pure virgin, not a harlot.

11
The Ultimate Headache

The Day of Pentecost was the day godly Jews gathered to remember the giving of the Law on Mount Sinai. On that day they offered their harvest to God. They remembered that deliverance came to Israel after they ate unleavened bread. In fact, Israel was forbidden to even have leaven in their homes.

Jesus warned that leaven was indicative of the poisonous doctrine of the Pharisees (see Matthew 16:12). Their great error was that they made the Law vain, didn't see sin in its true light and therefore saw no need of the One who would redeem them from the curse of the Law. Had they not made the Law ineffectual, they would have accepted Him as the Deliverer from its wrath. They even hindered others from entering God's

Kingdom because of this: "Woe unto you, lawyers! for you have taken away the key of knowledge: you entered not in yourselves, and them that were entering in you hindered" (Luke 11:52, KJV).

The lawyers were professing experts of the Law. But they didn't use the *key of knowledge* to bring the knowledge of sin, as a schoolmaster to bring sinners to Christ. They hindered its work: "For the priest's lips should keep knowledge, and they should seek the Law at his mouth: for he is the messenger of the Lord of hosts. But you are departed out of the way; you have caused many to stumble at the Law" (Malachi 2:7-8).

With those thoughts in mind, let's continue the comparison of the harlot of Proverbs 7 and her dealings with the youth, and modern evangelism's method of dealing with sinners. The harlot's means of capturing this unthinking youth was one of seduction--with "fair speech she caused him to yield, with the flattering of her lips, she forced him" (vs. 21). Paul deliberately refrained from enticing speech in seeking those who would be part of the Bride of Christ (see 1 Corinthians 2:1). His preaching was free from seduction of any sort (1 Thessalonians 2:5). The marriage supper of the Lamb will not be a "shotgun" wedding. A true marriage is when the bride and groom give themselves to each other *willingly*. When Ruth sought a husband in Boaz, she came to his feet and asked for the covering of his mantle. She came *willingly* and submitted to his covering.

Bridal Assistance

If you are seeking a bride for a friend, and you feel you must turn down the lights, make an emotional plea for a commitment, physically assist the bride down the aisle, then plan to follow her closely to make sure she keeps her marriage vows, it doesn't exactly compliment the husband. *The inference is that you have an ugly friend.*

Through seduction, the harlot *caused* the youth to yield. That seems rather strange. Most unregenerate men don't need to be *forced* into bed with a beautiful woman. *The Amplified Bible* tells us of the inner conflict of sin and the conscience. It says that with the allurements of her lips she leads him to "overcome his conscience and his fears."

The youth's response to her seductions is immediate (vs. 22), and so is the response of the false convert. He "immediately" receives the seed into his heart (see Mark 4:5).

The alluring lips of the pleading preacher, the

long altar call, the soft music, the draw-card counselors, and the gospel of happiness, make him ripe for the plucking. He lacks knowledge of what he is doing. He begins to build and cannot finish.

The youth of Proverbs, chapter 7, doesn't understand that what he is doing will cost him his life, and neither does the false convert realize that he is trifling with the eternal destiny of his very soul. When Esau despised his birthright, it was no small thing in the sight of God (see Hebrews 12:16).

In his ignorance to the gravity of his sin, the false convert despises his blood-purchased birthright. He doesn't value the precious blood spilled on Calvary's Cross. He tramples underfoot the blood of Jesus Christ to appease the sensuality of his flesh.

He connects himself to the Harlot church, and becomes one flesh with her, showing himself "to be neither fit for the land, nor yet for the dung-hill." He cleaves to her until the sharp arrow of God's Law strikes his liver, when God says, "You fool, tonight your soul shall be required of you."

What's Wrong With This Picture?
Those who truly love God perceive the shadowy practices of the Harlot church. They

know that things are not right. They perceive that somehow the many who have taken on the name of Jesus Christ under her seduction, don't match up to the biblical standards of what a Christian should be. They find it difficult to rejoice with the crowd when masses of sinners respond to the altar, merely because more numbers have named the name of Christ. They know that there are many who came through that same door, and now their latter end is worse than the first. They discern that the Harlot church "has cast down many wounded" (vs. 26). There is no joy in drawing "water from the wells of salvation," when the bucket is filled with holes.

The man of the world smiles with delight when he introduces a youth to an experienced hooker, because he knows he will enjoy the stolen waters of sex with a prostitute. But the insightful observe that "hooker" is an appropriate word. They see the tragedy of a youth going in to a prostitute. In doing so, a young man is destroying his very soul.

The student of Scripture knows how grievous it is that Satan has wounded so many through a false conversion. Their spiritual state is now worse than before their decision. But the full tragedy will not be known until Judgment Day, when it will be seen that "her house is the way to Hell, descending to the chambers of death."

The Seductive Mantle

In Judges 4:18-21, Jael covered Sisera with a mantle, and when he thirsted she gave him milk to drink. Then, when he had gone to sleep, she took a nail and drove it through his temple and killed him.

The demonic spirit behind the Harlot church wants to cover the unsuspecting convert with the mantle of deception. She wants a decision from him. Then she will give him the "milk of the Word," but rarely the strong meat, and especially not the Law of God. Like a babe, he is kept "unskillful in the word of righteousness." She deceives the heart of the simple. It is the Law that "makes wise the simple" (Psalm 19:7), so he is kept in ignorance of the Law. When he settles down to sleep in the darkness of his ignorance, when false peace embraces him, *she drives the nail into his slumbering temple to bring about his untimely death*.

The spirit puppeting the Harlot church is the spirit of antichrist--the spirit of the "lawless" one (see 2 Thessalonians 2:8-12). False converts have a "strong delusion," that they should "believe a lie."

The delicate warm mantle of the Harlot church is not the fine linen of the righteousness of the saints, but the sinful shroud of Hell. Her house *is* the way to Hell, descending into the chambers of death.

The word used for the proverbial "harlot" is *zanah,* conveying that this is a woman who is "highly fed and therefore wanton." Her god is her belly, her glory is in her shame, she minds earthly things. The Harlot church "fares sumptuously." Scripture also communicates the thought that she commits adultery "rarely of involuntary ravishment." In other words, her harlotry is deliberate and willful.

I am convinced that the harlot of Proverbs, chapter 7, and the rich man Jesus spoke of in Luke 16:20, are two types of the same thing (this we will see in a future chapter). It would seem that both are types of the false church, made up of false converts, false apostles, false prophets, and false teachers, who have a false sense of assurance of eternal security. This shouldn't surprise us. Paul spoke of false apostles who were deceitful workers, that transformed themselves into the apostles of Christ. Then he said, "And no marvel; for Satan himself is transformed into an angel of light. Therefore it is no great thing if his ministers also be transformed as the ministers of righteousness" (2 Corinthians 11:13-15).

Light to the Straight-gate

How can we keep "youths" from being deceived by the seductions of the Harlot church? The answer is in Proverbs 6:23-24: "For the Commandment is a lamp; and the Law is light; and reproofs of instruction are the way of life. To keep you from the evil woman, from the flattery of the tongue of a strange woman."

The light of the Law shows the sinner the path of life in Christ, and warns him of the Harlot, not to go "astray in her paths." Those who rightly divide the Word of Truth know that "reproofs of instruction *are the way of life*." The schoolmaster, the God-given instructor, gives light to the straight and narrow gate, so that he doesn't enter the wide way of destruction.

The Hebrew harlot's access to the youth was his lack of understanding, and it is also a lack of understanding that gives the spirit of deception access to the mind of the sinner. God's Law *produces* knowledge. Understanding lifts up her voice and cries out in the gates: "To you O men, I call, and my voice is to the sons of men. O you simple ones, understand prudence, and you fools, be of an understanding heart" (Proverbs 8:4).

God likened Israel to a harlot in Jeremiah 3:3, saying that she had a "harlot's forehead." A harlot held her head high in pride, when she should have bowed low in shame. When seeking a customer, she would cover herself with a mantle as a virgin bride covers herself with a veil in a sense of innocence and modesty (see Genesis 38:14). The harlot covers herself with a counterfeit purity and false humility.

The Harlot church is proud of her achievements, yet like the smug Pharisees, she puts on an air of piety and humility. In her heart she is like Diotrephes, who loved "to have the preeminence" (3 John 1:9). She veils her true intentions, promising pleasure without the commitment of being "espoused to Christ." She is built on lust rather than love, and passion rather then purity. She never had a first love to leave. She is a puppet, a free expression for the spirit that works in the children of disobedience. Like Judas, she professes to follow Jesus, but would betray him for 30 pieces of silver. She will raise her hands in worship, then betray the Son of God with a kiss.

Jerusalem was supposed to be "the faithful city," but God said that she became a harlot (see Isaiah 1:21). Look at her unfaithfulness to her God: "But you trusted in your own beauty, played the harlot because of your fame, and poured out your harlotry on everyone passing by who would have it. You took some of your garments and adorned multicolored high places for yourself, and played the harlot on them. Such things should not happen, nor be . . . yet, she multiplied her harlotry in calling to remembrance the days of her youth, when she played the harlot in the land of Egypt" (Ezekiel 16:15-16; 23:19).

When God espoused Israel, cleansed her wounds and covered her with "fine linen," all He wanted of her was her faithfulness to the Law, yet so often she proved to be a whore at heart (see Ezekiel 16:10).

12

The Contraceptive Pill

Israel continually backslid from the Lord. She perpetually broke the Ten Commandments. She failed to understand that God required "truth in the inward parts," and therefore lacked the fear of Him. The first result of this was that she became self-indulgent and lawless (see Jeremiah 8:10). Second, she preached a false peace (vs. 11). Third, she lacked contrition (vs. 12). The producing of contrition is a primary function of the Law, as it shows sin as being exceedingly sinful, to the end that there might be "godly sorrow" which "works repentance unto salvation." Fourth, the result of lawlessness among God's people was a lack of fruit (vs. 13).

What was the answer for Israel? It was the light of understanding, that in sinning she had "sinned against the Lord" (vs. 14). Her sin was that she had transgressed His Law, something made clear in Jeremiah 7:9: "Will you steal, murder, commit adultery, swear falsely, burn incense to Baal, and walk after other gods whom you do not know . . . ?" Through this verse we can see that they had broken the 1st and 2nd Commandments by having a false god, the 3rd in that His name was therefore blasphemed among the Gentiles because of their sin, the 4th because their idolatry violated the Sabbath, thus breaking the 5th and dishonoring their parents. They transgressed the 6th through murder, the 7th through adultery, the 8th through theft, the 9th through false witness and the 10th by coveting the gods of other nations.

The modern church is no different. There are multitudes who are in a state of "perpetual backsliding." They are like Israel of old, who "flattered Him with their mouth, and they lied unto Him with their tongues." They draw near to God with their lips, but their hearts are far from Him. They profess that they know God, but in works they deny Him, being abominable, and disobedient, and to every good work reprobate (see Titus 1:16).

They haven't been given the Law, so they do not repent before God. They proceed to walk in the imagination of their own heart, and become self-indulgent and lawless. The fact that they are still in their sins is seen in that they are not redeemed "from every lawless deed" (Titus 2:14). What's more, the Harlot church continues to say there is peace "when there is no peace." At the first mention of the name of Jesus on his lips, the convert is told he has peace with God, yet Jesus warned that we are only His friends *if* we do what He tells us (see John 15:14). We are only His disciples, if we continue in His Word (see John 8:31-32). The spurious convert uses grace the same way a fornicator does a contraceptive pill. He still sins, but thinks he will never suffer the consequences.

The Planting of the Lord

There is also a deficiency of fruit in the Harlot church--the fruit of righteousness, fruit of holiness, fruit of praise, fruit of thanksgiving, fruit of repentance, and fruit of the Spirit. Why? Because they are not "the planting of the Lord," they are the planting of man. They are not "born of God," but of "the will man." Jesus warned, "Every plant, which my heavenly Father has not planted, shall be rooted up" (Matthew 15:13).

"But," you may say, "I didn't have the Law

preached to me when I came to Christ." Let me ask you a few questions. When you came to the Savior, did you have a knowledge of sin? You must have, or you would not have repented. He who repents turns from sin, and "sin" is transgression of the Law (see 1 John 3:4).

What then was your sin? Was it lust, adultery or fornication? If so, then your sin was that you transgressed the 7th Commandment. Did you steal (8th), hate (6th), lie (9th), or blaspheme (3rd)? Were you covetous (10th), were you selfish or ungrateful to God? Did you realize God should be first in your life (1st, 4th)? Or maybe you suddenly discerned that God was nothing like you thought He was (2nd). Did you feel bad about your attitude to your parents (5th)? How did you know that you had sinned against God? Wasn't it because you knew of the Ten Commandments? Someone, somewhere, somehow, had said to you "You shall not kill, You shall not steal," etc., and your conscience bore witness with the Law. Like Paul, you too will say, "I had not known sin, but by the Law" (Romans 7:7).

There is the prevalent thought that the Church is falling short of what it should be, because there are many within it who have failed to make Jesus "Lord" in their lives. Yet, a Christian *is* a person who has made Jesus Lord. If Jesus is not "Lord," then who is? Jesus said, "He that is not with Me is against Me; and he that gathers not with me scatters abroad" (Matthew 12:30). No man can serve two masters.

The Harlot church fails to be salt and light, *because she isn't salt and light.* She refuses the Lordship of Jesus Christ, because she is the Harlot. Those who don't understand this will be forever criticizing the Church rather than seeing what the real problem is, and with the help of God, exposing it. Chaff is always disappointing. It has no body to it. It is forever being blown about. If this isn't understood, it will be a mystery as to why so many "Christians" support television preachers who are obviously false prophets. These charlatans don't preach Christ crucified, the necessity of repentance, the Law of God, the inevitability of judgment, or the fear of God. They merely preach prosperity, and they prosper themselves because of the support given them by those we think should know better.

Rather, these individuals are chaff who are "blown about by every wind of doctrine." The fan of God's judgment will reveal the true from the false. He will thoroughly purge His threshing floor, and gather His wheat into the barn; but He will burn up the chaff with unquenchable fire (see Matthew 3:12).

13

Friends Not Enemies

Unfortunately, many think that Law and grace are opposed to one another. This may be because of the typical translation of John 1:17: "For the Law was given by Moses, *but* grace and truth came by Jesus Christ." The word "but" is not in the original, and when translated without its negative connotation, shows that they don't oppose, but harmonize: "For the Law was given by Moses; grace and truth came by Jesus Christ."

When originally translated in the eighteenth century, the Law's function was common knowledge, but readers of the Scripture in this century read something dissenting into it, something which was never intended.

The Scriptures are full of harmony between the Law and the gospel:

"Though your sins be as scarlet (Law),
they shall be as white as snow (gospel)"
(Isaiah 1:18).

"Come unto me all you that labor (Law)
. . . and I will give you rest (gospel)"
(Matthew 11:28).

"If any man thirst (Law), let him come to
me and drink (gospel)" (John 7:37).

"For the letter kills (Law), but the spirit
gives life (grace)" (2 Corinthians 3:6).

"For if the ministry of condemnation
(Law) be glorious, the ministry of
righteousness (grace) exceeds much more
in glory" (2 Corinthians 3:7,8).

Like blind Samson, the Church has been
seduced by a harlot (see Judges 16:1). It has lost
the strength it once had. But God is raising up
ones who will take that blind Church and place its
hands firmly upon the pillars of the two tablets of
the Law. As we learn to open up the spirituality of
the Commandments and let the weight of eternal
justice fall upon sinners, they will flee from the

wrath that is to come. Three thousand died under Samson's strong hand, and three thousand also died when the strength of the Law did its work at Pentecost. It nailed them to the Cross of Calvary. The Law was a schoolmaster to bring them to Christ.

Two Donkeys

In Matthew 21:2, Jesus sent two disciples and said, "Go into the village opposite you, and immediately you will find a donkey tied, and a colt with her. Loose them and bring them to Me." Notice that there were *two* donkeys--a mother and a colt with her. The New Testament then tells us that this happened that it might be fulfilled which was spoken of by the Old Testament prophet, saying: "Tell the daughter of Zion, 'Behold, your King is coming to you, lowly, and sitting on a donkey, a colt, the foal of a donkey.'"

Then the disciples "brought the donkey and the colt, laid their clothes on them, and set Him on them." Again, notice the reference to two animals.

In Mark 11:4, Jesus told two of His disciples that they would find the two animals "in a place where two ways meet." This was the beginning of the culmination of the ages. That which was to take place over the following days would be when "two ways" would meet. "Righteousness and peace" were about to kiss each other in the Messiah. The Law came by Moses, but grace and truth were being revealed in Jesus Christ. Moses made manifest the Law of Eternal Justice, but in Jesus Christ all flesh would see the salvation of our God.

Zechariah combined the lowly donkeys with justice and salvation in his prophecy of this incident. He said: "Behold, your King is coming to you; He is just and having salvation, lowly and riding on a donkey, a colt, the foal of a donkey" (Zechariah 9:9). Both Law and grace carried the Messiah to Calvary.

The Cross was made of two sections, fastened together as one. With one part taken away, there could be no cross. One was fixed horizontally, and one stood tall and vertical. The Law was the level of holy equity. The perfect balance of the scales of Eternal Justice came to rest, satisfied at the Cross. The grace of our God found root in the earth, and upheld the Law as a testimony to a sinful world throughout the ages.

Law and grace were responsible for the lowliness of His incarnation, and both found perfect harmony in the atonement of the Cross of Jesus Christ.

Friends Not Enemies

It was the rod of Moses that struck the Rock of Jesus Christ. It was because of the Law that He was "smitten of God, and afflicted." The hand of grace made the Rock produce the waters of everlasting life for dying humanity.

The great burden of the stone of the Law has been rolled away by the grace of God. Now we have direct access to the risen Savior.

The irreversible decree of the Law throws us into a den of ten devouring lions. Grace stops their mouths.

The wrath of the Law chases us to the edge of the Red Sea. Grace opens the waters.

Grace is the loving hand that covers the eyes of Moses, so that the Glory of God may pass by and not consume us.

Getting the Fax

I was trying to fix our fax machine, when it rang. I picked it up and found that it was a young man named Brian who had dialed our fax number by mistake. Before he hung up, I told him to read his Bible. When he said he was a Catholic, I said that the Bible said he had to be born again. He replied, "I don't need that, man." So we went through the spirituality of the Law, and the fact of Judgment Day. His reaction was interesting. He said, "$@#!!@*! I never heard it put like that

before! *I had better think this one out.*" That's
what the Law does. It gives the blind sinner light,
information . . . an ultimatum.

The day before, I had spoken to another young
man who said that he had never heard the claims
of the gospel before. Interestingly enough, he said
he was familiar with John 3:16. When we are true
and faithful witnesses and preach the whole
counsel of God, it gives sense to John 3:16. The
light of the Law is the brilliant star that leads us
to Bethlehem's Savior.

A respected German theologian of the last
century said:

> Both the Law and the gospel must be
> preached, the one in its sternness, the
> other in its sweetness. A preacher who
> does not preach both, does not deserve
> the name of an evangelical minister, but
> is a false leader and is sowing the gospel
> as if he were casting wheat into the
> ocean, where no crop can be raised.

Delighting the Heart of God

The character of God cannot be separated from
His Law. Justice and judgment are the habitation

of His throne (see Psalm 97:2). We can catch a tiny glimpse of God's love for justice, when Solomon asked God for wisdom in 1 Kings 3:10-13. His request so delighted God, He told the king that He would give him long life, if he would keep the Law. Then comes the famous narrative about two women, both claiming to be the mother of one child.

Solomon demonstrated God's wisdom by commanding that the child be cut in two, thus exposing the true mother from the false. It is interesting to note that both these women were harlots (see 1 Kings 3:16). The Chaste Virgin was once "foolish, disobedient, deceived, serving divers lusts and pleasures . . . But after that the kindness and love of God our Saviour appeared" (Titus 3:3-4, KJV). Like Rahab the harlot, she found grace in the sight of God. She trusted in the scarlet thread of the Savior's blood, and found cleansing from the corruption of her sin.

These two women dwelt in the same house (vs. 17). Both the true and false convert dwell side-by-side in the House of the Lord. Each of them called Solomon "lord." Both the Harlot church and the Chaste Virgin call Jesus "Lord." Therefore, it takes the wisdom of Solomon to discern the true from the false.

What was it that showed Solomon the genuine mother from the deceiver? The real mother manifested true love. She would rather lose her child than see it cut in two by a sword.

Here is wisdom: *the Harlot church will show her spirit by, without hesitation, dividing the Body of Christ in two, rather than making withdrawal in humility.* She will cut a body of believers in half because of a pet doctrine. She sows discord among the brethren. Her proud wisdom is not from above, it is not easily reasoned with.

Yet, the Chaste Virgin will immediately back away from a contention that divides a local church. She knows that "the beginning of strife is as when one lets out water" (Proverbs 17:14). She places her battles in the hands of Him who says "vengeance is Mine." She "leaves off contention," and commits herself to "Him who judges righteously," because she has wisdom that is primarily peaceable.

Hundreds of times in Scripture, God refers to Himself as "*the* Lord your God." However, the Chaste Virgin is like Thomas who touched the hands and the side of Jesus. When he did so, he cried, "*My* Lord and my God." The Virgin knows the price she has been bought with. She has looked on Him who was pierced. Like Thomas, she has seen His wounds, and she fully knows they are there *because of her sin*. She has seen Jesus Christ "evidently set forth and crucified." She has presented her body as a living sacrifice, holy and acceptable to Him. That is her reasonable service. She is not conformed to this world, because she has been transformed by the renewing of her mind. He is her Lord and her God.

In this humble yielding to the way of the Spirit, she is seen to be the "true mother." She strives for the unity of the gospel. She knows that she has passed from death unto life because she loves the brethren, and therefore will go to great pains not to offend a brother. She won't even eat meat if it causes another to stumble. Her prayer is the prayer of the Savior, that they all may be one (see John 17:21). She remembers that Joseph said that his brethren wouldn't see his face until they had their brother Benjamin with them. She wants unity of the brethren so that the face of Jesus can be clearly seen in her by the world.

Often the spirit of the Harlot isn't clearly manifested. Like the twins in the womb of Tamar who played the harlot (see Genesis 38:1-30), both the true and false convert may look identical, but the Christian is the one with the "scarlet thread"

139

of the blood of Jesus Christ "bound upon his hand." The twins of the true and the false may look alike, but God knows the difference, He knows those who are His. They are the ones who have departed from "lawlessness" (see 2 Timothy 2:19). They have the hope of grace because they are as "obedient children," not fashioning themselves according to the former lusts of their ignorance. They have purified their souls in obeying the truth (see 1 Peter 1:14-22).

14

Doing its Job in Israel

Why did so many flock to John to be baptized? The answer is given in Luke 16:16: "The Law and the prophets were until John: since that time the Kingdom of God is preached, and every man presses into it." (KJV) The Law gave Israel the "knowledge of sin." They were instructed as to the exceedingly sinful nature of sin. They knew of the righteousness of God, the holiness of God, and the wrath of God, *because the Law was doing its job in Israel.* That's why so many flocked to John for the baptism of repentance.

Similarly in Matthew 11:12-13: "And from the days of John the Baptist until now the Kingdom of Heaven suffers violence, and the violent take it by force. For all the prophets and the Law prophesied until John." (KJV) What made the Kingdom of

Heaven suffer violence? Why did the violent take it by force? The answer is in verse 13. It says *For*. In other words, *this is the reason*: "For all the prophets and the Law prophesied until John."

A man who doesn't believe he's drowning will make no effort to be rescued. But if he suddenly believes he is about to perish, he will desperately make an effort to be saved. In fact, a drowning man will even become violent in desperation, to a point where the lifeguard may have to knock him unconscious, so he can get him to the safety of the shore.

The Law makes a man desperate. It shows him that he is drowning in sin. It makes Hell reasonable, and like Felix (see Acts 24:25), he trembles. It shows him, not only that Hell exists but that he is in great danger of going there, making him cry out, *"What must I do to be saved?"* The glad tidings of mercy are only glad tidings to those who understand the bad tidings of judgment. The Law is the brush which paints a clear picture of Hell in the mind of the sinner. The Law lets Hell's fire burn in his guilty conscience. He embraces the gospel the same way a man who is about to drown seizes a lifesaver, or as a man in the final throes of a terminal disease grasps the cure. *Give me the cure when I don't even know I have the disease, and I won't hold on to it with any conviction.*

Low Fat High Energy Diet

John the Baptist prepared the way of the Lord. That's what the Law also does. It prepares the way so that the course to the Savior will be made plain. The valley of decision is made smooth. The preacher who seeks only the praises of God, like John, should ingest a balanced diet of the locusts of the Law and the wild honey of the gospel. The gospel becomes positively sweet to those who have been plagued by the Law.

Herod's adulterous mouth was stopped because John preached the Seventh Commandment (Luke 3:19). Preach the Law, and the Harlot will want your head "on a platter." Light produces heat, and the heat was too hot for Herodias. But we are not to fear those who can kill the body, and afterwards can do no more. The swift and sharp executioner's sword severed more than the head of John from his body. It cut him loose from this cursed earth and ushered him into eternal glory.

John's death was a forerunner of what would happen to the Church. Jesus said that it was expedient that the Head should be taken from the

Body of Christ, so that the Holy Spirit could come. Now, because of the empowerment of the Spirit, he that is least in the kingdom of Heaven is greater than John. We can preach the same Law that John preached. We can point to the One whose sandle-straps we are not worthy to unloose, and we can do so in the power of the same Spirit that raised Christ from the dead.

The sad thing about many men of God is that they see from Scripture that the Law brings the knowledge of sin. They see that it is holy, just, and good, and that it was the schoolmaster that brought *Israel* to Christ, *but they don't see its potential evangelistically*. One day in July of 1982, as I studied the Epistle to the Romans, the thought suddenly flashed into my mind, "I wonder if the Law can be used to bring the knowledge of sin nowadays, as it did in Israel so long ago?" So I went out with the Law in hand, and tried it on a sinner--and to my surprise, *it worked!*

Then I studied the gospel proclamation of Wesley, Whitefield, Spurgeon, Luther, and others, and found that they all strongly advocated the Law to prepare the way for the gospel. They upheld it as the only means by which a man can find the knowledge of sin, and therefore find genuine repentance.

144

Doing its Job in Israel

You Need to Know

A typical modern-day evangelistic statement is "Jesus is the way to Heaven. You need to have that assurance that you are going there when you die." This is true. However, if a sinner responds to the gospel solely to get assurance of Heaven, and not to flee from God's wrath, *which he realizes he deserves,* then he will be a prime target for the Harlot.

Would the woman caught in the act of adultery have been driven to the feet of the Savior if reference hadn't been made to the fact that she had transgressed the Law, and therefore should come under its wrath? If she hadn't been saved from its fury by Jesus, she would have, no doubt, gone her way and sinned some more.

Some may seek to justify a grace alone gospel with Romans 2:4, saying that it's the "goodness of God" that leads us to repentance. Their thought is, all we need to do is speak of God's goodness, rather than His wrath, to bring men to Christ. In one sense they are right. The effect of doing so should reveal transgression of the Law. God freely lets the rain fall on the just and the unjust. He pours His blessings of life, liberty, love, laughter, sunshine, friendship, food, sex, the blessing of children, color, music, snow to ski on, sea to swim in, the sun to warm us, the wonders of nature to delight our hearts, and flowers to brighten the days. With all the goodness of God manifest in the blessings of this life, it is our reasonable service to have God first in our affections, to love Him with all of our heart, mind, soul, and strength. But what does humanity do? We spit in His face by using His name to curse. We hate God without cause. We are rebels. We are children of disobedience, unthankful, unholy, lovers of pleasures more than lovers of God--*incredibly ungrateful*. We are weighed in the balance of the First Commandment and found infinitely wanting. His goodness *should* bring us to a point of obedience, and it is the Law that shows us how "wanting" we are.

When modern preachers speak of the goodness of God, they confine His "goodness" to His love, His mercy, and His wonderful grace. They limit the virtues of His character. God's goodness is also manifest in His justice, righteousness, holiness, and His fearful indignation against sinful man. A judge is "good" if he hates crime and seeks to bring evil men to justice. If Paul in Romans 2:4 was speaking of the goodness of God as merely His love and mercy, saying that is the essence of our message, then he wasn't practicing what he was preaching. Read Romans, chapter 2, and you will see that the verse is sandwiched in terrible wrath, pure Law, and fearful Judgment.

Double Deception

To what was Jesus referring to when He said not to cast pearls before swine? To what was He pointing when He said not to give that which is holy to the dogs, lest they trample them under their feet, and turn and tear you in pieces (see Matthew 7:6)? The most precious pearl the Church has is "Christ crucified." Preach grace to the proud and watch what they do with it. They will trample the blood of the Savior under their feet with their false profession, and, what's more, they become enemies of the gospel. If not physically, you can be sure they will tear you in pieces verbally. They do "despite to the Spirit of grace." That means they insult the Holy Spirit. "Bitterness" and "backslider" are bad bedfellows for the Church. The proselyte becomes a two-fold child of Hell.

Those who make a profession of faith, without having a humble heart (which the Law produces) have the experience: "According to the true proverb, 'The dog is turned to his own vomit again; and the sow that was washed to her wallowing in the mire'" (2 Peter 2:22). This is the tragic result of casting pearls of the gospel of grace to the proud, or what the Bible calls "dogs" and "swine."

The false convert has never "crucified the flesh with its affections and lusts." He, like the pig, must go back to wallowing in the mire. Pigs *need* to wallow in mire because they crave the slime to cool their flesh. So it is with the false convert. He never repented, so his flesh is not dead with Christ. It is instead burning with unlawful desire. The heat of lust is too much for his sinful heart. He must go back to the filth.

Only Believe

Sadly, there are still those who think they can be more effective in evangelism by preaching a "believe and repent" gospel. This is despite the biblical order of preaching repentance first, then faith (see Acts 20:21). The "only believe" message is attractive because it has little offense, and it seems to reap a greater harvest. The thought is, when the person has joined the company of believers, *then* he can learn about repentance. This method came into being because the Law had been dropped from gospel proclamation. Those who don't see the function of the Law fail to see the absolute necessity of repentance *and therefore think that their convert is saved, when he is not*. He has had a spurious conversion if he has not repented (see Luke 13:3; Acts 3:19). It is quite understandable that the "convert" has not repented, *because he hasn't been told to*. He has just "believed." The truth is, he *cannot* repent if he doesn't know what sin is, and as we have seen, the Law is the only means of knowing what sin is (see Romans 7:7).

The deception comes as a result of both the convert and the preacher thinking he is saved because of his spiritual experience of a new life-- joy, gladness, and faith. Yet *these three things accompany the experience of the false convert--the stony ground hearer* (see Mark 4:16; Matthew 13:20). The Bible says that the false convert, for a while, *does* actually "believe." However, he believes "in vain" (see 1 Corinthians 15:2). There is a *genuine* false conversion experience.

Again, because the Law hasn't been employed to show sin in its actual light, there is no understanding of its nature and therefore no contrition--"The Lord . . . saves such as be of a contrite spirit" (see Psalm 34:18; Isaiah 57:15; 66:2).

So the sinner settles down in his false

assurance of salvation. He has new friends, new principles to live by, a better marriage, a conquered drug or alcohol problem--a new life. Granted, there are those who, under the teaching within the church, come to a point of what is commonly called a "recommittal." But if this is the *first* sign of biblical repentance, then it is not *recommittal*, but salvation from sin. He has been born again while seated among God's people.

Fruitless Trees

A man in his mid-sixties who, after hearing the teaching of the use of the Law in evangelism, said that he had "led about seventy people to the Lord" during his lifetime. This was the first time he had ever heard of the teaching. Then, wide-eyed, he expressed deep concern that his eight children had all made a profession of faith, and yet he couldn't see an ounce of the work of regeneration in their lives. In the light of "every tree that does not bring forth good fruit will be cut down and cast into the fire," he had good reason to be concerned.

I would dare say, most preachers who think all is well with modern evangelism, more than likely don't personally witness of their faith. I know from experience that it is easy to get so busy ministering that it's hard to find time to do one to one witnessing. But I make the time to do so, and I have lost count of how many people I have heard use language that would make your ears tingle, or admit they were into fornication, and then say, *"Oh, I'm a Christian, I've been born again."* Sometimes one doesn't need too much discernment to distinguish between the mantle of the Harlot and the fine linen of the Chaste Virgin.

The world is full of caustic "backsliders" *who never stayed within the church building to get the teaching they were supposed to get*. When trouble came to the Harlot, she shook her fist at the Heavens. Her thirst was only for pleasure, and when God didn't deliver, she followed her heart's desire and went back to drinking iniquity like water.

An even greater disaster than people falling away from their commitment to the church, *is the fact that multitudes of unrepentant "believers," stay within its midst*. These rest in their "conversion experience," and unless they are awakened by the Law, they will do so until they cry, "Lord, Lord," and be cast from the doors of Heaven into the jaws of Hell.

15

Good Enough For Jesus

There was once a general who sent his army to fight a war. To ensure that they had courage while fighting and to make sure they won the war, he decided he would issue them ten great cannons. The enemy was terrified when it heard that the battle would involve these massive weapons. So in great subtlety, they infiltrated the army and convinced those in a place of leadership that the cannons were far too heavy to carry. They maintained that, in time, the cannons would wear down the soldiers, and that they would be better to replace them with handguns.

So that's what the leaders did. All this took place without the knowledge of the soldiers. Consequently, when the infantrymen went into battle, they were fearful because the handguns were little protection from the weapons of the enemy. Of course, the soldiers were of little threat in modern warfare. In time, they became the laughingstock of the enemy, and very little of the adversary's territory was taken.

It was then that a number of infantrymen found the general's original strategy, and discovered how the enemy had cheated them out of their greatest weapon. Moved with a sense of indignation, they recovered the ten cannons and rushed into battle, filled with new-found courage.

That's what the use of the ten great cannons of the Ten Commandments can do for the soldier of Christ. Instead of the enemy looking like giants, they look like grasshoppers. The sinner no longer laughs at the gospel when it comes on the heels of the Ten Cannons of the Law. Instead, he lifts his hands in submission and comes across to the winning side, never to become a deserter.

The person who is saved through the spilled blood of the Messiah, becomes a Chaste Virgin unto Christ, and the very thought of going back to the sinful world grieves him. He knows that to do so, he would have to trample under foot that precious blood.

Put That Down

In 1982, after reading a small portion of gospel

proclamation by Charles Spurgeon, I began to study the function of the Law and, for the first time, saw its great purpose. It was as though God looked down on my frustrated efforts and saw me in the heat of battle, fighting against the strongholds of the enemy with a lightweight shotgun. In His mercy, He leaned forward and said, "Put that down. In My Word, you will find the weapons of warfare I have provided. They are not carnal, but mighty for the pulling down of strongholds." I looked at my War Manual and saw the Ten Great Cannons of the Commandments, and the immediate effect was that courage filled my heart. I went back into battle with renewed enthusiasm. But more than that, instead of the world laughing and mocking me, I found that they lifted their trembling hands as they looked down the massive and loaded barrels of the Law, and said, "I surrender all . . . all to Jesus I freely give."

Much to my delight, I found that those who enlisted in the army of God didn't turn from the holy commandment.

To encourage you into battle with renewed zeal, we are going to take a look at different aspects of the ten majestic Cannons of God's Law, particularly in reference to how to practically discharge them.

Some preachers don't actually quote the Ten Commandments when, and if, they feel to use them. As far as they are concerned, they are simply a part of the Bible. They don't despise the Law, but they don't see the necessity to use them as the main arsenal. To them I would like to give ten good reasons why we should *specifically cite* the Law, rather than make a general reference about it being wrong to lie, or wrong to steal, etc., when we are witnessing or preaching.

For years Christian leaders have been speaking about the fact that we have forsaken the "Judeo-Christian ethic." It's as though the nation was dying of thirst, but no one would actually pinpoint the fact that "water" was the answer. Their vague "Judeo-Christian ethic" *is* the Moral Law. Why should we specify this Law? Here are ten reasons:

1. Jesus saw the necessity to precisely quote the Commandments:

"You know the Commandments, Do not commit adultery, Do not kill, Do not steal, Do not bear false witness, Honor your father and your mother" (Luke 18:20). *Even though His listeners knew the Law*, Jesus still took the time to actually quote each Commandment: "You have heard that it was said by them of old time, You shall not kill" (Matthew 5:21). "You have heard that it was said by them of old time, You shall not commit adultery" (Matthew 5:27). "He said to him, 'Which ones?' Jesus said, 'You shall do no murder,' 'You shall not commit adultery,' 'You shall not steal,' 'You shall not bear false witness.'" (Matthew 19:18). "*You know the Commandments*, Do not commit adultery, Do not kill, Do not steal, Do not bear false witness, Defraud not, Honor your father and mother" (Mark 10:19, italics added).

The fact that Jesus saw the need to *literally quote* the Law should be abundant reason for actually declaring the Commandments. Look at how James follows the example: "For He who said, Do not commit adultery, also said, Do not murder. Now if you do not commit adultery, but you do murder, you have become a transgressor of the Law" (James 2:11).

Paul also did the same: "For this, You shall not commit adultery, You shall not kill, You shall not steal, You shall not bear false witness, You shall not covet; and if there be any other Commandment, it is briefly comprehended in this saying, namely, You shall love your neighbor as yourself" (Romans 13:9).

These in themselves should be sufficient. However, let's look at some more grounds for actually quoting each of the Ten Commandments when preaching or witnessing:

2. When the Commandments are quoted, they carry an authority.

They are absolute. When the Law isn't specifically cited, what is our point of reference when we say that it's wrong for someone to steal? Their moral perception becomes relative. If the world has no moral absolutes, it is because the Church has failed to *show* this people their transgressions; and "sin is transgression of the Law."

3. God gave Moses the Law twice in exactly the same (quoted) form in the Old Testament.

4. God promises an anointing on His Word.

The Ten Commandments are pure Scripture--they are therefore "quick and powerful and sharper than a two-edged sword," and should be preached as they are written.

5. Other religions say it is wrong to steal, lie, to kill, to commit adultery, etc.

Their points of reference are the writings of men. The Ten Commandments are unique because they are God-given . . . written by the finger of God (see Exodus 31:18), therefore their content and origin should not be at all adulterated.

6. The Bible says, "The work of the Law is written on their hearts"
(Romans 2:15).

Each of the Ten Commandments is written on the conscience. The conscience will affirm that God is just in His demands. Every sin against the Law has been recorded on the tables of their heart: "The sin of Judah is written with a pen of iron, and with the point of a diamond: it is graven upon the table of their heart, and upon the horns of your altars" (Jeremiah 17:1).

To thoroughly teach them, with the view of converting the soul, is to work with the Holy Spirit, who convicts the world of sin . . . which is transgression of the Law (see 1 John 3:4), righteousness . . . which is of the Law (see Romans 8:4), and judgment . . . which is by the Law (see Romans 2:12; James 2:12). "You shall not steal" is the Commandment written on stone, and "You shall not steal," etc., (personal, unbending, absolute) is written on the heart.

In March of 1991, a man on the East Coast of the U.S., shot a turkey and put it in the trunk of his car. Unfortunately, the not-quite-dead bird revived while in the trunk and began to kick its legs. Its foot hit the trigger of the gun, which went off and hit the man in the leg. When the incident became public, the turkey hunter found himself with a stiff fine on his hands, because it took place two weeks before the beginning of turkey shooting season.

The Law revives the conscience. It puts kick back into what seemed to be dead, so that the sinner's transgression will be brought into the open: "Once I was alive but quite apart from and unconscious of the Law. But when the Commandment came, sin lived again" (Romans 7:9, *The Amplified Bible*).

7. Satan hates the Law, and will therefore give a preacher every (unbiblical) reason not to use it.

Martin Luther, when speaking of using the Law as Paul did . . . as a "schoolmaster to bring us to Christ" said, "This now is the Christian teaching and preaching, which God be praised, we know and possess, and it is not necessary at present to develop it further, but only to offer the admonition that it be maintained in Christendom with all diligence. *For Satan has attacked it hard and strong from the beginning until present, and gladly would he completely extinguish it and tread it under foot.*" (italics added)

8. *Why not* quote the Commandments?

Which one is unreasonable? Take each Commandment at face value. Every one of them makes sense. Even the Commandment that is used by the Seventh Day Adventists to try and bring us back into bondage, is logical. While there is no New Testament Commandment (or even a hint of a command) to keep the Jewish Sabbath Day holy, it makes sense to work for six days, then rest on the seventh. Any nation that forsakes that simple principle will, in time, suffer from stress.

9. When a man steals, lies, or commits adultery, his great error is that he thinks he has merely broken man's law.

To him, sin is horizontal. To say it is merely *wrong* to steal, to lie, to kill, etc., is to leave him in that delusion. He must be shown that his crime is *vertical*. Until he understands that fact, he will fail to repent before a holy God, whose Law he has violated. He may make a decision to change his lifestyle and become part of the Church, but transformed though he may be, unless he repents, he will perish.

10. If we don't understand the function of the Law, that it is "good, if it is used lawfully" (1 Timothy 1:8-9), then our own natural thinking will be offended by it.

We will want to set it aside because "the carnal mind is enmity against God: for it is not subject to the Law of God, neither indeed can be" (Romans 8:7, KJV).

To make it a witnessing or preaching habit of citing the Ten Commandments is to guard against leaning towards the natural reasoning mind, rather than the spiritual. It is a safeguard against being drawn into a way of preaching to which the carnal mind and the world approves.

Charles Spurgeon said, "The Law with its ten black horses drags the plowshare of conviction up and down the soul from end to end of the field, till there is no part of it left unfurrowed. And deeper than any plow can go, conviction goes to the very core and center of the spirit, till the whole heart is wounded. The plowers make deep furrows indeed when God puts His hand to the plow. The soil of the heart is broken in pieces in the presence of the Most High."

You may choose to use only one horse of the ten supplied, but in doing so you will prolong the plowing of the field. Just as God gave ten utterances in Genesis to bring about the Adamic creation, so He gave ten utterances of the Law to bring sinners to the new creation in Christ.

In April 1996, a Dallas pastor preached the gospel at a funeral of an unsaved man. Hundreds of mostly secular people packed his small church building, overflowed into the hallway and even into the parking lot. Before he presented grace, he took the time to go through each of the Ten Commandments one by one, opening up the spirituality of the Law of God. He thoroughly plowed the field before sowing the seed.

After the funeral, even though he felt he had been faithful to God, thoughts began to invade his mind that perhaps he was too harsh. How could he speak of Judgment Day, when the family was hurting so much after the loss of a loved one!

However, the following Sunday, ten people (including a number of relatives of the dead man) came to the pastor's church. They were unsaved, but they appreciated what he had said enough to come back. They that sow in tears, will reap in joy.

On June 26, 1876, a certain general in the U.S. Cavalry was leading his troops towards a coming battle. Unfortunately, he made three great mistakes:

1. He underestimated the strength and number of the enemy.

2. He thought that his soldiers were eager to get into battle because their horses rushed forward. However, they were actually inexperienced riders who couldn't control their horses. His last recorded words to them were, "*Hang on there boys, there's enough Indians for all of us.*"

3. He cut two gattling guns loose, saying they were slowing down the progress of the troops.

General Custer and modern evangelism have much in common.

16

Wine Into Water

Many Christian organizations do *everything but* use the Law to bring the "knowledge of sin," and consequently have to put great emphasis on something contemporary evangelism calls "follow up." One very well-known and respected preacher, whose evangelism program has exploded world-wide, said his policy attempts to get at the heart of the fall away rate of new converts "by placing great stress on the follow up."

Sadly, this common and unscriptural concept is a testimony to the lack of confidence modern evangelism has, both in its power of its message and in the keeping power of God. If God has saved them, God will keep them: "He is able also to save them to the uttermost," to keep them from falling, and "present them faultless before the presence of His glory with exceeding joy." If He is the author, He will also be the finisher of their faith, and if He has begun a good work in them, He will complete it. Jesus said if the Father gives ones to Him, then "no man is able to pluck them out of my Father's hand" (John 10:29). If God has had no part in their salvation, then they are not in His hand, they are still in the hand of the devil.

When pastor and author, David Wilkerson called me after hearing a message called "Hell's Best Kept Secret," the first thing he said was, "I thought I was the only one who didn't believe in follow up!" A new convert should be fed, discipled, and nurtured. This is biblical and most necessary, and if he has come with an understanding of sin, like the Ethiopian eunuch, he will not have to be followed. He will put his hand to the plow and never even look back, because he is "fit for the Kingdom" (Luke 9:62). If they are born of God, they will never die, if they are not "born of God," they can never live, no matter how much we follow them.

By "follow up," I mean when laborers have their energies re-directed to those who have made decisions. Their job is to be their "life-support." The worker then becomes familiar with having to call and say, "I didn't see you at church last week," or "Are you reading your Bible?" etc. He has the ministry of encouragement, and after being involved in the follow up ministry, he will need encouragement himself.

The true convert will get into fellowship *because* he is a disciple of Christ. He will desire the sincere milk of the Word because he is told to. He will not need to be coerced, manipulated, or pressured to grow. If he is saved, he will keep himself in the love of God, and continue in the Word of Christ. He will take up his cross and deny himself daily. If he has been truly saved, he will delight to do those things. He doesn't do these things *to* be saved, he does them *because* he is saved. He has a new heart by which God causes him to walk in His statutes.

If you study the Parable of the Sower, you will see that it was the sunlight of persecution and temptation which exposed the false convert. But, as we looked at earlier, in the case of false converts who are pampered with follow up, the soft pillow of deception is placed under his head. He doesn't live godly in Christ Jesus, therefore persecution doesn't expose his fraud. He has surrendered to sin, and therefore doesn't have a battle with temptations of the world, the flesh, and the devil.

Bride of Heaven, Pride of Hell

The spurious convert is further tucked into the cradle of falsehood by being told that he should never question or doubt his salvation. This teaching is directly opposed to Paul's command to examine ourselves and see if we are in the faith (see 2 Corinthians 13:5). He who is about to jump 25,000 feet from a plane does well to thoroughly check that his parachute is firmly intact.

A Mountain of Fertilizer

Imagine if I came to you with a dilemma. My garden has 90% of its crop break through the soil, but it withers and dies as soon as the sun begins to shine on it. I make sure it gets enough water and fertilizer and I know the seed is good quality. I have even gone to the trouble of propping up each plant with small sticks as it comes out of the soil, but all to no avail.

You would more than likely encourage me to check the soil. I need to take a shovel and turn it over, *before* I plant the seed. You are familiar with the stony area in which I am planting, so you advise me to take the time to thoroughly dig over the earth, and remove the many stones that are obviously stopping any depth of root. It really doesn't matter how much water or fertilizer I put *onto* the soil, the problem is unseen . . . *in* the soil. Once the ground is clear of obstacles, the sunlight will then benefit it by giving the plant a thirst, causing it to send its roots in deep, rather than causing it to wither and die.

Here is our problem. Up to 90% of the evangelistic crop is failing. They wither and die as soon as the sunlight of tribulation, persecution and temptation shines on them. We encourage them to be watered by the Word. We give them the "fertilizer" of counsel and support. We follow them up thoroughly, but all to no avail.

So, we then need to check the soil. If, *before* we plant the seed of the gospel, we take the time to thoroughly turn the soil of the heart with the Law, the effect will be the removal of the stones of sin upon repentance.

God has given us insight into the area in which we are planting. The ground of the human heart is very hard. The Scriptures call it a *stony* heart (see Ezekiel 36:26).

I have heard a number of household name preachers say that it is biblical normality to have 75% of those coming to Christ, fall away. During the altar call, they know that only one in four of those responding to their message will go on in their faith. So, they are more than likely not too alarmed by modern statistics which reveal an 80%

failure. The basis of this thought is that the Parable of the Sower shows that only 25% of the crop was on good soil (see Mark 4:1-20). But I am convinced that Jesus didn't give the parable as a consolation for disappointing evangelistic results, but for our instruction. When we study the parable closely, we see that the good soil hearer, the *genuine* convert, had some things the other hearers didn't have. He had *understanding* (see Matthew 13:23), and he had a *good and honest heart* (see Luke 8:15). Does that mean that throughout humanity, there are those who somehow have understanding and a good and honest heart, and we have to keep on sowing until we find them? No, Scripture makes it clear that there is *none* who understand (see Romans 3:11), and that the heart of man is not honest, but deceitful and desperately wicked (see Jeremiah 17:9).

How then did the genuine convert obtain these necessary virtues? Something from *outside* of his own heart must have *given* him understanding and *brought him to a point* of having a good and honest heart. The *schoolmaster* taught him that his heart was wicked. The shovel of the Law turned the soil and exposed the stones of sin. When these were removed through repentance, it left the good soil of understanding, and a heart that saw itself in truth.

Those with a "good and honest heart" are merely those who are poor in spirit, who are honest about their own wickedness. Their mouth of justification has been stopped by the Law (see Romans 3:19). They can now receive the incorruptible seed of the Word of God, and it will bring forth fruit without hindrance. They are "born again, not of corruptible seed, but of incorruptible, by the word of God, which lives and abides for ever" (1 Peter 1:23). These are the ones who go their way and sin no more (see 1 John 3:9).

This was the key to the success of men like George Whitefield. These men thoroughly prepared the soil of the heart with the Law, *before* planting the seed of the gospel. Look at Whitefield's wisdom regarding fall away: "That is the reason we have so many 'mushroom' converts, because their stony-ground is not plowed up; they have not got a conviction of the Law; they are stony-ground hearers."

Again, it is the shovel of the Law that turns the soil, so that it is no longer a "stony heart," but a "good and honest heart." The stones of rebellion against God are cast away, so the convert can bring forth fruit with patience. Then once the soil is clear, the seed of the gospel should grow unhindered. The sunlight of tribulation, temptation, and persecution will benefit rather than hinder growth. Any plant, if it is on good soil, will send its roots deep into the earth when the heat of the sun shines upon it. Those who take the time to "sow in righteousness," will "reap in mercy;" but they must first "break up the fallow ground" with the Law.

The use of the Law in evangelism does not guarantee the salvation of souls. It is God alone who makes a seed grow, and without the work of the Spirit, there is no life in the soul who hears the Law. It is not the rope that saves a drowning man, but the one who holds the other end of the rope and pulls him to the safety of the shore. God is sovereign in the salvation of sinners. Repentance is God-given (see 2 Timothy 2:25), the act of repentance is the obligation of the sinner (see Acts 17:30), and the Law is the instrument God has given to bring this about.

Bloody Mary

It was Thanksgiving of 1995 and I was on a plane heading for Chicago. On one hand I felt blessed, but on the other hand I felt a little frustrated. Blessed, because I had two steward-esses standing in the aisle and pleading for more gospel tracts. Our claim is that our tracts are so unique, people ask for more . . . and here was proof. I began by showing them our optical illusion tracts. These are so fascinating, a scientist once saw them and said, "My brain is melting!" Then I followed with three IQ card tracts, which also do weird things to the human brain, trailed by our eye-widening "Wallet." The stewardesses were so excited, they returned later and said the other members of the crew are asking, "Who is this passenger who is so much fun?" Then they said, "This is so neat. What can we do for you? Would you like a beer, a 'bloody Mary' or some white wine?" I told them I was a preacher, and if they gave me wine I would probably just turn it into water. I had the new wine of the Holy Spirit.

However, on my right hand I wasn't so blessed. There sat a woman who listened intently as I went through the Ten Commandments, but after I explained the Cross, she told me that she was a Moslem. She didn't need Jesus, because when she sinned, all she had to do was confess to God that she was truly sorry, and He forgave her. I told her that a judge in a civil court can't just forgive and release a criminal because he is sorry. He is bound by the law to see that justice is done. Her answer was reasonable from a human viewpoint. She said that the judge couldn't forgive because he couldn't see if the criminal was truly sorry. God could see the heart and therefore He forgave the genuine penitent. To her, He didn't need a basis to forgive, because He is God.

I went back to Abraham and explained that God required the shedding of the blood of an animal as a justification for His forgiveness, and explained that Jesus was the Lamb of God, and without Him there was no salvation. Even though she listened, and loved the tracts, her reaction was strange. She held out her hand and asked if I could read palms. I told her I couldn't, and preferred reading Psalms. To an on-looker, I had wasted my time.

Even though it was tough going, my confidence was that God saves whom He will, whether they are professing atheists, self-righteous church-goers, Moslems, or stubborn Jews on the road to Damascus. If God's hand is upon that woman, the Law will begin to weigh heavy upon her, and bring her to the foot of a blood-stained Cross. There is no other way to procure salvation but through the Savior, because only Jesus can say, "Peace, be still" to the storm of God's Law. Only His blood can calm the hurricane of God's wrath and the sea of His fury. That woman needed the leading and guiding of the Holy Spirit of Truth. All that God required of me, was to be a true and faithful witness.

17

No Looking Back

After God spoke of the New Covenant, He said that those who would be saved *would not* backslide: "And I will give them one heart, and one way, that they may fear Me for ever, for the good of them, and of their children after them: And I will make an everlasting covenant with them, that I will not turn away from them, to do them good; but I will put my fear in their hearts, *that they shall not depart from me*" (Jeremiah 32:39-40, italics added).

Bible commentator Matthew Henry said that it was quite legitimate to interpret this as a promise to those in Christ. I agree with him. The "one way" we have been given is in Jesus Christ. It is the fear of God which causes those within the New Covenant not to depart from the Lord. The true convert puts his hand to the plow and doesn't look back for the same reason Lot's wife shouldn't have looked back. The fruit of salvation is that "they may fear (God) forever." That is the missing ingredient in modern evangelism's converts because it is the missing ingredient in modern Christendom.

In years past, I took great consolation in the fact that countries like Korea were having a "move of God," with literally hundreds of thousands responding to the gospel. Unfortunately, from what I've seen, the decisions have been made from a Lawless gospel and consequently they *need* to be followed up. A well-known Korean pastor thought it amusing as he said, "We have cell leaders contact them (church members) on Saturday night, and *pull* them to Church." The ministry of prop-up will only last until Judgment Day.

Other successful churches, because of their large numbers, used to be a source of encouragement, until I gained insight into their evangelistic methods. In recent years many pastors from these churches have fallen from grace, through adultery. In fact, *Christianity Today* found, in a confidential survey among 300 pastors in the U.S., that nearly one in four had been involved in some sort of sexual sin. This happens because of a lack of the fear of God.

It is natural to want to have a charitable attitude and believe that a brother who leaves his wife and runs off with his secretary is merely a Christian who has fallen. We may even be able to justify this thought with a few Scriptures. However, in the light of a mountain of other Scripture, we mustn't discard the fact that there is such a thing as false conversion. The Bible says, "Hereby we know that we know Him, if we keep His commandments. He that says, I know Him, and keeps not His commandments is a liar, and the truth is not in him" (1 John 2:3-4). "Whosoever abides in Him sins not: whosoever sins has not seen Him, neither known Him" (1 John 3:6).

The human heart has a bias to sin. We are more likely to keep on the straight and narrow path if we understand the principles of counterfeit conversion, rather than fostering a belief that grace gives us a license to sin. Antinomianism is nothing new. It has long been Satan's subtle strategy. In the early Church, he had certain men who "crept in unnoticed . . . who turned the grace of God into licentiousness" (Jude 4).

Martin Luther, in his commentary on

Galatians, wrote of demonic doctrines that were invading the Church of his day. Look at this satanic cunning which left him aghast in unbelief: "Satan, the god of all dissension, stirreth up daily new sects, and last of all, which of all other I should never have foreseen or once suspected, he hath raised up a sect as such as teach . . . *that men should not be terrified by the Law, but gently exhorted by the preaching of the grace of Christ."*

Read his words again. They perfectly sum up much of modern preaching . . . they are gently exhorted by the preaching of the grace of Christ. Think of Luther's words in respect to the average altar call.

John MacArthur said, "God's grace cannot be faithfully preached to unbelievers until His Law is preached and man's corrupt nature is exposed. It is impossible for a person to fully realize his need for God's grace until he sees how terribly he has failed the standards of God's Law. It is impossible for him to realize his need for mercy until he realizes the magnitude of his guilt. As Samuel Bolton wisely commented, 'When you see that men have been wounded by the Law, then it is time to pour in the gospel oil.'" (*John MacArthur New Testament Commentary*, Matthew 19).

Life Support

At a concert in Salt Lake City in 1991, people were challenged by a well-known and respected gospel musician to accept Jesus to get "power." Literature was given to the counselors warning that it was normal to have a 95% fall away of those responding to the message. The counselors were told that they would become the new converts' "life-support system." They, not God, were responsible for keeping them in the faith. Sadly, if the converts responded to get power rather than to repent, they may be on a life-support system, but they are brain dead.

Many churches are bursting at the seams with converts, who do nothing but attend church on Sunday. They are not burdened in prayer or hungry for the Word. Neither do they live in holiness or have any concern for the lost. They are not at church to be equipped for war so that they might do the will of God, they are there to sit on a pew for an hour or so, and even then they must be entertained or they will lose interest.

The Scriptures tell us: "'Behold, the days are coming,' says the Lord, 'when the plowman shall overtake the reaper, and the treader of grapes him who sows seed; the mountains shall drip with sweet wine, and all the hills shall flow with it'"

(Amos 9:13). There is biblical evangelism. One plows the soil of the heart with the Law, before sowing the seed of the gospel. The other reaps. He who sows and he who reaps, rejoice together. One treads out the grapes of the wrath of God, while another sows the seed of the Word of God, so that the mountains then drip with the sweet new wine of the life of God in Jesus Christ.

Carrying Your Converts

If someone makes a decision to trust the Savior, and you find that you have to carry them in their Christian walk, you may have a "Mephibosheth" on your hands. As a baby, this offspring of one who had fallen from grace (King Saul), was carried by a nurse. In her haste to save the child from the enemy, she stumbled, dropped him, and did serious injury to his feet, which left him lame.

The contemporary church, in her haste to try and save souls, is doing great injury to her converts. Without the knowledge of sin and the consequent act of repentance, her offspring are never able to get on their feet spiritually, and will find themselves stumbling in and out of the world.

18
Stop or I Will Arrest You!

When Peter realized who Jesus was, he said, "Depart from me Lord, for I am a sinful man." This is true contrition. Peter understood that he was poor in spirit, as Isaiah did when he "saw the Lord." Each man had a sense of unworthiness. He suddenly perceived that this was the God of Abraham, Isaac, and Jacob, manifest in the flesh. This was the God who revealed Himself in thunder and lightning to Moses as He gave him the Law. *This was the Holy One of Israel.*

Jesus of Nazareth was the embodiment of everything the Law stood for . . . truth, righteousness, holiness, justice, goodness, and perfection. In front of this sinful fisherman stood the glory of the only begotten of the Father. This was the One of whom "Moses, and the Law and the

Prophets spoke." This was the true light, and the effect was a revelation of the darkness of sin. Why? Because Peter was a Jew, and despite his apparent ungodliness, he had knowledge of sin, which must have come through the Law.

The Advantage of the Jew

The apostle Paul asks the question, "What advantage then has the Jew, or what profit is there of circumcision? Much every way! Chiefly, because to them were committed the oracles of God" (Romans 3:1-2). Right in the middle of his discussion about the Law, Paul tells us that the Jews had great advantage over the Gentiles, in that the Law had been committed to them by the very mouth of God.

The Hebrew word used for oracles is, *utterances,* or as *The Amplified Bible* aptly puts it, the "brief communications" (see Deuteronomy 4:7-13). The Ten brief oral communications told the Jew what sin was, knowledge the Gentiles didn't have. This is why Paul so often used the phrase "to the Jew first": "For I am not ashamed of the gospel of Christ: for it is the power of God unto salvation to every one that believes; *to the Jew first, and also to the Greek*" (Romans 1:16,

186

italics added, KJV). "But glory, honor, and peace, to every man that works good, *to the Jew first, and also to the Gentile"* (Romans 2:10, italics added).

In 1 Corinthians 1:23, Paul makes a difference between response to the gospel, by Jew and by Gentile. He says, "But we preach Christ crucified, to the Jews a stumblingblock and to the Greeks foolishness." Why didn't he say, "We preach Christ crucified, to both the Jews and Greeks foolishness"? What is the difference between the way a Jew heard the gospel, and the way a Greek received it? The difference was the Law.

The Greeks thought Christ crucified was foolishness, or an absurdity, because they were ignorant of the Law, had no knowledge of sin and therefore saw no need of the Savior. Why did they need a cure when they weren't diseased? The fact of someone paying a fine on my behalf is absurd, when I don't believe I have transgressed any law.

However, the Jews had a knowledge of the Law of God, and yet stumbled over the Cross. It was an offense to the Jew *who had a proud heart*, but to those who were humbled by the Law, Nicodemus, Nathaniel, and the devout Jews on the Day of Pentecost, the gospel became the "power of God unto salvation." It gave light to their darkened minds.

Badge of Authority

In 1989, when we, as a family, came to the United States, I was preaching at Venice Beach, California, where unbeknown to me at that time, the police wore shorts and rode around on bicycles. When I stood on a soapbox and began to speak on the edge of the wide sidewalk, a crowd of about 80 people gathered around to listen. Suddenly, a man in shorts stood right in front of me and told me to stop. When I ignored him, he became very indignant and told me once again to stop. I asked, "Are you a police officer?" He then smoked at the nostrils and said through gritted teeth, *"If you don't stop right now, I will arrest you!"*

It was then that I noticed a badge on his belt, which told me he *was* an officer of the law. Suddenly, his words carried a lot of weight! I was elevated above him, and his badge was out of my sight, so I had no respect for him other than that which I would give an ordinary civilian.

Those who are representatives of the Living God, yet don't point to the Law as the core of their authority, will not gain due consideration from the world. Jesus stood before the multitudes as One who was a representative of the Law of God. The Bible says the Messiah would bring justice to the earth and that the "coasts shall wait for His Law" (Isaiah 42:4). He repeatedly referred to the Law as the point of His authority, saying, "I have not come to do away with the Law," "Not one jot or tittle of the Law shall fail," "This is the Law and the prophets," "Have you not read in the Law?" "It is easier for Heaven and earth to pass away than for one tittle of the Law to fail." (Matthew 5:17-18; Matthew 7:12; Luke 16:17).

For the Church to neglect to point to the Law of God, is to hide the badge of our authority from the world. Understandably, they will disregard what we have to say. The gospel we preach is only there because God stands by the holiness of the Law. If eternal Law didn't exist, then there would have been no need for a sacrifice. The Law *demands* retribution. It was the Divine fire of God's Law that fell on the sacrifice of Calvary.

If the world knew that there is an Eternal Law that they must face, that that Law necessitates death and Hell for transgression, then they would seriously consider the claims of the gospel. If they understood that the long arm of the Law will reach right down into the heart of humanity, they would repent. If they *knew* that Almighty God is "smoking at the nostrils," that His wrath abides upon them, they would flee to the Savior. When speaking of God's Law, Charles Spurgeon said, "Having thus removed the mask and shown the desperate case of the sinner, the relentless Law causes the offense to abound yet more by bringing home the sentence of condemnation. It mounts the judgment seat, puts on the black cap and pronounces the sentence of death. With a harsh unpitying voice it solemnly thunders forth the words *'condemned already!'*"

Dust Free

Perhaps you are tempted to say that we should never condemn sinners. However, Scripture tells us that they are *already* condemned (see John 3:18). All the Law does is show them their true state. If you dust a table in your living room and think it is dust free, try pulling back the curtains and letting in the early morning sunlight. You will more than likely see dust still sitting on the table. The sunlight didn't create the dust, *it merely exposed it*. When we take the time to draw back the heavy and high curtains of the holy of holies and let the light of God's Law shine upon the sinner's heart, all that happens is that the Law shows him himself in truth. The Commandment is a lamp and the Law is light. Again, it was the wrath of the Law that showed the adulterous woman that she was condemned. She found herself between a rock and a hard place. Without those heavy rocks waiting to pound her sinful flesh, she may have died in her sins and gone to Hell. I doubt if she would have fallen at the feet of Jesus, without the terror of the Law having driven her there. Thank God that it awakened her, and caused her to flee to the Savior.

The sinner thinks that he is rich in virtue, but the Law shows him that he is morally bankrupt. If he doesn't declare bankruptcy, the Law will mercilessly call for his last drop of blood.

The Ceased Human Heart

There is no room for error. We are surgeons in the emergency room, operating under the sacred anointing of the Great Physician. We are to use the scalpel of the Law to cut away the flesh, and transplant new hearts into this dying world. We are firemen, braving the fires of persecution, beating down the doors of sin with the sharp ax of the Law to rescue sinners from the flames of Hell. We are paramedics applying the two stone tablets of the Law to jolt the ceased human heart into the life of Christ. We are officers of the Law, holding back the advancement of crimes against the God of Heaven, calling for those who will surrender themselves to the mercy of the judge, while there is yet time.

While Men Slept

We have had many letters from Christians who find a new fearlessness in witnessing because they now have the Law as a weapon. They feel cheated that the enemy hid such a powerful weapon from their sight. One who typified the reaction said, "Why has this biblical principle fallen to the wayside? *It infuriates and grieves my heart I was never taught this before!"* Another letter said, "I had never seen anyone respond to the gospel message before . . . now everyone responds! Let me tell you not all responses are good. That's O.K."

The cannons remove the smoke of apathy from the battlefield. The Commandments clear the air, demanding some type of response. No longer can a sin-loving sinner shrug off the gospel by saying, "I'm quite happy as I am thanks," because happiness is no longer the issue. The Law shows him he is a Hell-bound rebel against the God who gave him life, and without righteousness, he will be damned forever. It is no wonder the devil hates God's Law when it is used lawfully.

There is a veil over the eyes of those to whom God gave His Law, regarding grace; and there is also a veil over the eyes of those to whom God has given grace, regarding the lawful use of the Law. In Matthew 13:25-41, we see that the reason the enemy infiltrated the Church with lawless "converts," was because "men slept." Somehow the devil rocked the Church to sleep around the end of the nineteenth century. There was a divorce in the marriage of the Law and the gospel. That which God had joined together, he separated, and then he began to sow tares to his devilish heart's delight.

Law without grace is the needle without the thread, the syringe without the liquid, the shell without the gunpowder. They need each other to be effective. The thunder and lightning of the Law should always precede the lifegiving rain of the gospel. One without the other allows the enemy to sow tares.

The Law and Liberty

When the world throws off what it thinks are the "shackles" of the Ten Commandments, they don't find liberty, they find bondage. They took the Law from the walls of the schools, and they wonder why this generation kills, lies, and steals without any qualms of conscience. Hate manifests itself through teenage neo-Nazis, sexual license brings disease and guilt, sending suicide rates sky-rocketing. What else can we expect when *You shall not kill, You shall not steal, You shall not lie* has been removed from their sight. If you remove all the signs of the law from a freeway, you will sanction lawlessness. Even with the restraint of warning signs reminding motorists of the lawful speed of what they should and shouldn't do, many motorists live on the edge. They strain at the bit of restraint. If *all* indication of the law was eliminated, every man would drive according to his own rule, and the result will be chaotic.

On the other hand, paradox though it may be, the restraining of the Law brings liberty. A lawful football game is a game unhindered by trans-gression. It will flow without restriction. A lawful society is a society free of drug abuse, crimes of passion, adultery, murder, rape, hate, theft, etc. The only way to bring about a Law-full society is through revival. This is when God writes His Law on the hearts of a generation. When that happens, the whole generation dies. Its evil Adamic nature is killed by the Law. The Law means death to the guilty (see Romans 7:1,10). The Hebrew word for the ark in which the two tablets of the Law were contained, was *arown,* meaning "coffin." Paul calls the Law "glorious" in 2 Corinthians 3:7, referring to it as "the ministration of death, written and engraven in stones."

When the Law is kept, it produces liberty. This is why James calls it the "perfect Law of liberty" (James 1:25). It liberates a society from the bondage of sin, through the death of the vehicle of sin, the Adamic nature.

19

Our Aim Under God

Let's now look briefly at the role of music during an altar call. To do this, we will go back to the antique vase spoken of in an earlier chapter. My son broke a $25,000 vase I told him not to touch. Imagine if I said, "Son, you have just broken a $25,000 vase I told you not to touch! Do you see the seriousness of what you have done? *Are you sorry for doing something I told you not to do?* Before you answer, let me put on some soft music to help you make up your mind."

If I did that, I would move away from his will and conscience, the area at which I should be aiming. I would move into the field of his emotions. I can't shed a tear for my neighbor's salvation, but I find myself with great drops in my eyes while watching a sad TV program. I have found that the moment I turn the volume down on the television, I am able to take control of myself. The music stirred my emotions.

Our aim, under God, is to stir the conscience and the will. Music, *played during a call to decision,* may stir an emotional response and get a sinner to the altar, but when he comes down from being caught up in the moment, his heart is still in the world. Music can move mountains, but it cannot remove sin from the human heart. Obviously, it has a legitimate place in worship, but it is a great error to use it to stir the emotions to get a response to the gospel.

I remember renting a movie called, "So Many Voices." I thought it would be applicable for a family night at our church. I hadn't seen it, but I trusted it would be suitable for family viewing.

The night of the screening, the hall was packed with families. The movie started with a man walking at night through a graveyard. The music was at such a pitch, one just knew that something awful was about to happen. The atmosphere was electric. All you saw was this man's boots as he moved from tombstone to tombstone in the dark of the night. As the camera slowly moved up the torso of this shadowed stranger, the mood moved to terror. I could feel the fear in the room. Then I had the added horror of the thought, *"What have I done . . . this was supposed to be a family night!"*

The picture then focused on the face of this fearsome figure. As it did so, he stuck his tongue out and did what is commonly called a "raspberry." The crowd burst into laughter. The man smiled, then explained that this movie was about the effects of music on the emotions of the human heart. He illustrated its effect by showing the same scene of the man moving through the graveyard, but this time it was accompanied by marching band music. As the "fearsome" figure moved from tombstone to tombstone, everyone in the hall burst into laughter, which continued throughout the whole scene.

It was an invaluable example of how music can shape the human response. It is a lesson every evangelist and pastor should be familiar with, because evangelistic tradition has dictated that it is almost a sin not to have soft music during an altar call.

In one sense, modern evangelism has trapped itself into the necessity of having music during the call to the altar. When the Law isn't used to show sin in its true light, few *run* to the altar, broken, contrite, undone . . . *fleeing* from the wrath to come. There is no Holy Spirit conviction of sin, righteousness, and judgment in the meeting *because no sin has been uncovered by the Law*. So, the preacher reverts to creating an *emotional* response through music. If there is no music, there is no response, and the meeting is considered a failure.

It has been well said that our methodology betrays our theology.

The Morning Star

Remember, it was the Law that thoroughly prepared Saul of Tarsus for grace. He sat at the feet of Gamaliel, a respected teacher of the Law (see Acts 5:34). Without its instruction, he would not have known sin, nor would he have therefore known the Savior. That's why he said he delighted in the Law of God. The sinner who has been "taught according to the perfect manner of the Law of the fathers" will be stopped on the road to damnation. Like Saul, he will be blinded to the things of this world by the "light of the glorious gospel of Christ, who is the image of God."

The gospel light is brightest to those who have sat under the darkness of the Law. The black night of the Law is broken by the "Bright and

Morning Star." The air is wonderfully fresh after the rain, and the gospel is so pure after the down-pour of the wrath of the Law. Like Jonah's whale, the Law's purpose in swallowing the sinner, is only to change his stubborn mind about the things of God. Nineveh wasn't so bad after such a dark death experience.

There must be death by the Law before there is resurrection into the new life of the gospel. He who knows he has sinned against God, and yet has been given mercy, will be like humbled Saul of Tarsus and say, "Lord, what will you have me to do?" What's more, *he will do what his Lord says*.

A great preacher from the last century said, "When we preach the Law, it is not to make men saints, but sinners," and this is what Paul did at Ephesus when he preached against idolatry (see Acts 19:26). What do you suppose was his point of reference for their sin? It could only have been the Law of God which they had transgressed. When he preached to the Thessalonians, he also rebuked them for their transgression of the 1st and 2nd Commandments (see 1 Thessalonians 1:9).

What Else?

The lust of the flesh, the lust of the eyes, and the pride of life are the lifeblood of the nature of the unregenerate man. Like a dry desert, he soaks in evil like water. He loves darkness rather than light. For him to be born again, that adulterous sin-loving nature must surrender and be crucified . . . it must be hammered to the Cross. Just as Jesus went willingly to the Cross, so must the sinner come, saying, "Not my will but Yours be done."

Look again at the woman caught in the act of adultery. She was exposed by the radiant light of the Law. Its fury was about to crush her body and spill her sinful blood. She had no escape. Her only course was to throw herself at the feet of the Son of God and cry for mercy. Even though the Pharisees were talking to Jesus about the Law, we can only surmise as to what He wrote in the sand. Whatever it was, it brought a knowledge of sin to those who were so ready to stone that woman, to a point where they were convicted in their consciences. The "work of the Law" was written in their hearts. The conscience began to bear witness and accuse of sin. Billy Graham thought Jesus began to write the Ten Commandments in the sand. I tend to agree with him. They had been talking about the Law, and what else does God write with His finger?

Those who fall at the feet of the Savior, *after*

cowering under the shadows of the ten great boulders, know that if justice had been done, the Law would have crushed their guilty flesh back into the dirt from where it came. These are the ones, who, like the forgiven woman, listen to the command to go and sin no more. Yes, they hear the seductive voice of the Harlot, they see into her enticing eyes, they feel temptation rise like a fire in their soul, *but they fear Him who has power to cast both body and soul into Hell.* They know that if the eye causes them to sin, it is better to pluck it out and cast it from them, rather than go with perfect vision into Hell.

God has provided Ten Great Cannons for the battle against the demons of darkness. The Christian can now stand behind those great weapons and await the final victory. What a fool he would be to wander into sin and into their sights. The Bride of Christ knows that the lips of the Harlot "drip honey and her mouth is smoother than oil," but she is more "bitter than wormwood." The true convert sees that the Harlot "will hunt for the precious life." He understands that he cannot take fire to his bosom, against his fine linen, and it not be burned with the defilement of sin. His cry when tempted by the Harlot is, *"How can I do this thing and sin against God!"* But more than that. He knows the price of his redemption. He would not think of selling his birthright to everlasting life for the mere plate of red pottage, the temporal and warm appetites of the flesh.

The Outward Show

What if you use the Law, yet there is no sign of contrition? I have often had this experience, but I always remember that "salvation is of the Lord." We sow, somebody reaps, *but it is God who gives the increase.* I have seen sinners tremble under the Law, and I have seen them laugh at the Law. The ones who tremble aren't necessarily the ones who get saved first.

Often people will outwardly respond according to their temperament. A sanguine disposition may shed tears of sorrow far more readily than a choleric, and yet both are equally contrite. Felix trembled, but nowhere does it say he was saved.

Horizontal Repentance

A young man once heard the teaching of the importance of using the Law in evangelism and told me of a friend he "led to the Lord." This person didn't seem to have any evidence that he was saved, nor was he in fellowship with other

Christians. The dilemma was that he said his friend had actually repented, even though he had not used the Law to bring the knowledge of sin.

More than likely this person had mistaken sin as being horizontal rather than vertical. He repented because he had lied to and stolen from other people. He thought that "sin" was against *man* rather than against *God*. Yet, when David sinned with Bathsheba and broke all of the Ten Commandments . . . when he coveted his neighbor's wife, lived a lie, stole her, committed adultery, killed her husband, dishonored his parents, and therefore broke all the Commandments in reference to God . . . he said, "Against You, and You only have I sinned and done this evil in Your sight." How can a man repent *before* God, if he doesn't see that he has sinned *against* God. Paul preached "repentance *towards* God" (Acts 20:21). This was Joseph's theology when tempted to sin against Potifer by committing adultery with his wife. He said, "How can I do this great wickedness, and *sin against God!*" (Genesis 39:9). The prodigal son also had this revelation, and cried, "I have *sinned against Heaven.*"

Those who come to Christ in that spirit will reproduce of their own kind, and begin to bring about the ruin of the Harlot.

20

Vain Exorcise

If sinners come to Christ under the wrath of the Law, their repentance will be entire, vertical, and perpetual. This means they will not "give place to the devil." Many an hour has been wasted on exorcising a "brother" or "sister" of demonic activity, when the demons only have "place" because place was being given to them. A little digging finds that this professing Christian hates his mother or father. This almost guarantees a foothold for the enemy (see Ephesians 6:2-3). If there isn't transgression of the 5th Commandment, one of the others is being broken, for example, a "problem" with pornography, lying, hatred, or stealing, etc. Each problem usually traces itself right back to transgression of the Law.

Let me remind you of the context of the verse about resisting the devil:

> Adulterers and adulteresses! Do you not know that friendship with the world is enmity with God? Whoever therefore wants to be a friend of the world makes himself an enemy of God. Or do you think that the Scripture says in vain, The Spirit who dwells in us yearns jealously? But He gives more grace. Therefore He says, God resists the proud, but gives grace to the humble. Therefore submit to God. Resist the devil and he will flee from you. Draw near to God and He will draw near to you. Cleanse your hands, you sinners; and purify your hearts, you double minded. Lament and mourn and weep! Let your laughter be turned to mourning, and your joy to gloom. Humble yourselves in the sight of the Lord, and He will lift you up (James 4:4-10).

It would seem from the context, that Scripture is being addressed to "adulterers and adulteresses," those who are the enemies of God, to the proud, to those who have never drawn near to God, to sinners with unclean hands and impure hearts who look on sin lightly with joy and laughter. *These* are the ones who are being confronted . . . the ones who not only are in the world, but also dwell within the Church, who haven't humbled their hearts and submitted to God.

The Scriptures warn us to "walk in wisdom toward them that are without, redeeming the time." The Harlot church is without the Body of Christ, but she is still *within* the church building, and is used by the enemy to wear out the saints and tie up the laborers. Those who recognize her work, walk in wisdom toward her, and are, consequently, careful to whom they give their time.

Seven Signs

There was a great famine in the land of Israel. God was withholding rain. When David inquired of the Lord, he was told that the Gibeonites had the answer to the dilemma. They had been wronged and required some sort of "atonement."

"Silver and gold" would not provide recompense
. . . they wanted the death of seven sons of Saul.
The death of just any Israelite could not provide
atonement. So, seven sons of Saul were then
hanged on a hill.

The mother of two of the sons then put on
sackcloth, "spread herself on the rock" and kept
the "birds of the air" from feeding on the bodies
by day and the beast of the field by night. There
she remained from the "beginning of harvest until
the water dropped upon them out of heaven"
(2 Samuel 21:1-14).

There was a famine in the land. There had
been transgression of the eternal Moral Law. As
by one man sin entered the world, and death by
sin. So death passed upon all men, for all had
sinned. The whole of creation groaned in travail
under the searing heat of God's wrath. Heaven
withheld the waters of immortality. In time, death,
like a great famine, would starve the sinful sons
and daughters of Adam of life itself.

We had been weighed in the balance and found
infinitely wanting. God's Law required a sacrifice
to appease our transgressions, but no human being
could provide atonement (see Psalm 49:7). Eternal
Justice demanded neither "silver and gold, but the
precious blood of Christ" (1 Peter 1:18). God

Himself would provide the sacrifice. The offering of seven lambs could only provide temporal atonement (see Numbers 28:21), but the "Lamb without blemish or spot" came to earth and took away sin once and for all. By one offering He perfected them that are sanctified.

In this devoted mother of two of the men, we have seven signs of salvation:

1. Brokenness: In the light of the sacrifice, the Chaste Virgin (like the mother) is broken at the terrible cost of redemption.

2. Fear: She looks upon Him who was "hanged upon a tree" upon Calvary's hill (Acts 5:30), and trembles. She passes the time of her sojourning here in fear; *knowing* that she was not redeemed with corruptible things, such as silver and gold, but with the precious blood of Christ.

3. Humility: In the light of the sacrifice, the Church clothes herself in the sackcloth of humility.

4. Dependence: Moved by fear of wrath,

she spreads herself on the Rock of Jesus Christ (see 1 Corinthians 10:4). He alone is her foundation (see 1 Corinthians 3:11). He is her life.

5. Sanctification: She separates herself from her previous life. She so identifies with the sacrifice, she puts to death "her members which are upon the earth; fornication (Greek *porneia* or 'harlotry') uncleanness, inordinate affection, evil concupiscence and covetousness"

(Colossians 3:5).

6. Holiness: Neither will she allow demons ("birds," see Revelation 18:2) to feed on that which has already been crucified with Christ.

7. Passion for souls: The mother stayed "from the beginning of harvest until the water dropped on them out of heaven." Knowing the terror of the Lord, the Chaste Virgin persuades men. From the Day of Pentecost until the latter rain, she has seen that the fields are "white unto harvest," and her great desire has been for Heaven to rain down revival upon the earth.

The mother's name was "Rizpah," and means *live coal*. The Chaste Virgin has had her iniquity taken away and her sin purged by a live coal taken with tongs from the altar of God (see Isaiah 6:6). The burning coal has touched her lips. She cannot but speak that which she has seen and heard. She says, "Here I am Lord. Send me!"

21
How to Get 100 Decisions

How do you get children to come to Jesus? Simple. Just put one hundred of them in a room and ask how they can live forever. Someone will answer, *"You give your heart to Jesus!"* Ask who wants to live forever . . . one hundred hands go up. Now ask who wants to give their hearts to Jesus. There you have it, one hundred decisions. Most will put their hand to the plow until they become sexually aware, then you will lose them at 13, 14, or 15 years old.

Rather, we should see our responsibility is to "train up a child in the way he should go, so that when he is old, he will not depart from it"

(Proverbs 22:6). This is done by teaching them the Law (see Deuteronomy 6:4-9). This command came directly after the Ten Commandments were given (for the second time). How do you get a child to come to Christ? *You teach him the Ten Commandments*. This thought is horrifying to those who think this is an advocation of salvation by works. It is not. The Law *cannot* justify a soul. It merely leaves us guilty before God.

You tell children that if they tell a fib or a white lie they are transgressing the 9th Commandment and sinning against God. You teach them, "All liars will have their part in the Lake of Fire" (Revelation 20:8). You explain how taking something as insignificant as a ball point pen, which belongs to someone else, is theft. You tell them that it is wrong to be consumed by greed or what the Bible calls "covetousness." You point out how bad it is to have unclean sexual desires, to look at unclothed people, to be unfaithful in marriage. You teach that God created sex for marriage, and that fornicators and adulterers will not enter God's Kingdom. You explain that God sees our thought-life, that nothing is hidden from His holy eyes.

You also inform your daughter that she should dress modestly, that women who "dress to kill," are as guilty of breaking the Law as the men they cause to stumble.

You teach them that it is wrong to "get angry without cause," and "whoever hates his brother is a murderer." You show them that God requires them to honor and obey their parents, to faithfully attend church, and to honor God's name. They are to have a right understanding of His nature and character, which produces the fear of the Lord. You explain to them how God should be the focal point of their affections above all things.

You train up children in this way when you sit in your house, when you walk with them, and when you lie down with them (see Deuteronomy 6:7,9). You keep the Law between the frontlets of their eyes, explaining that God sees every hidden desire, requires an account of every idle word, and will bring to light every secret thing whether it is good or evil, on the Day of Judgment.

When they roam, the Commandments will lead them. When they sleep, they will keep them, and when they are awake, they will speak to them.

The War Against the Mind

As the child who has been taught the Law

grows, he is aware that only the "pure in heart shall see God," and becomes abundantly conscious that sin is at work within his members. He begins to cry: "Now if I do what I will not to do, it is no longer I who do it, but sin that dwells in me. I find then a law, that evil is present with me, the one who wills to do good. For I delight in the Law of God according to the inward man. But I see another law in my members, warring against the law of my mind, and bringing me into captivity to the law of sin which is in my members. O wretched man that I am! Who will deliver me from this body of death?" (Romans 7:20-24).

This cognizance of sin, combined with the knowledge that God is holy and will by no means clear the guilty, will drive him to the Savior. Here, he not only finds shelter from the wrath which is to come, but he also finds freedom from guilt, power over sin and death, and the warmth of the love of God he had only known in an intellectual capacity.

This has been the case with our literature with young and old. A number of our books have been written specifically aimed at the sinner, using the Law to thoroughly bring the knowledge of sin (see my books, *The Mystery*; *Comfort, the Feeble-*

minded; *The Secrets of Nostradamus Exposed*). In the middle of 1991, I went into a store and heard the man behind the counter using blasphemy. While serving a customer, he mentioned God so much I interrupted and said, "Excuse me. Is this a religious meeting?" He said, *"H–ll no!"* I said, "Yes it is, because now you're talking about Hell."

I went out to my van and got a copy of our book, *God Doesn't Believe In Atheists,* and gave it to him. Some weeks later, I gave him a copy of, *My Friends Are Dying!* Both these books use the Law to bring the knowledge of sin.

After a month or so, he called and told me he was cleaning out his room and was going to throw out *God Doesn't Believe In Atheists*, but instead opened it and began reading until he finished. He normally despised reading. Then he read *My Friends Are Dying* through completely, gave his life to the Savior, and went out and bought a Bible. Until the time of his conversion he was a practicing witch.

A Michigan woman in her mid 30's witnessed to her older sister a number of times over a 12 year period. Each time, she flatly rejected anything to do with the things of God. In January of 1996, the older sister contracted cancer. Once again she tried witnessing to her, but the dying woman still wouldn't listen.

Around that time the younger sister listened to our 16 audio tape series, which expounds principles of evangelism, and, in great detail, the importance of using the Law before grace. This time she took the time to take her sister through the Ten Commandments. The older sister had been very rebellious against her parents, and when she saw that the Fifth Commandment was "with promise" . . . long life, she widened her eyes. She then was able to understand that she had violated the Law and sinned against God. Life was no longer her "right." God owed her nothing but Eternal Justice. From there she found a place of genuine repentance, and died a few months later with the knowledge that she had already passed from death to life.

Twice, Twice.

Since the fall, man lost much of his brain capacity. They say we only use 10% of our brain. I could believe that. I would also go so far as to say that most men are a little slow on the uptake. One great principle of teaching is to tell a man what you are going to tell him. Then you tell him. Then you tell him what you told him. Still, most of us, only three days after being told something, forget 90% of what we hear . . . if I remember that statistic correctly.

I think it was in November of 1995 that *USA Today* published a list of things people forget most. Telling people things twice was high on the list. They are: names 83%, repeating things 49%, telephone numbers 57%, words 53%, repeating things 49%, faces 42%, directions 41%, and repeating things 49%.

Women tend to retain things more than men. In fact, men usually have to be told something twice. Ask any wife. Studies have shown that women speak twice as much as men. This is because men have to be told things twice (I may have mentioned that). This is something that seems to be substantiated by Scripture. When God spoke to men in the Bible, He said their names twice: "Abraham, Abraham" . . . "Moses, Moses" . . . "Saul, Saul" . . . "Samuel, Samuel." Perhaps Psalm 136 was written for men.

God doesn't repeat too much in Scripture, but He saw fit to give us the Ten Commandments *twice* (Exodus 20; Deuteronomy 5). He also instructed us twice about teaching the Law to our children (see Deuteronomy 6:4-8; 11:18-21) . . . I wonder why?

22
Hollywood Style

Someone may ask, "But isn't it the commission of the Church to preach the *gospel*, not the Law, to every creature?" True, that is our aim, but there is a right way and a wrong way to present the gospel. If I was instructed to fire an arrow, do I discard the bow to do so? The biblical manner to discharge the arrow of the gospel is to give it thrust with the bow of the Law of God. Granted, if you have a penitent sinner before you . . . a Nicodemus or a Nathaniel . . . then give him grace. But more than likely we will be surrounded by the proud, the arrogant or the self-righteous, where "every man will proclaim his own goodness" and be "pure in his own eyes." Why should an unenlightened, unregenerate person cry out, "What must I do to be saved?" if he doesn't see danger? The reason Nicodemus and Nathaniel were submissive was because, as godly Jews, the Law had humbled them. This was the case also with the devout Jews on the Day of Pentecost. They looked into the mirror of the Law, and were convinced by it that they were unclean.

There was once a movie in which a baseball scout found a young man with a lightning pitch. When he asked the youth's father if he could take him away to join a professional team, the father said, "See that church over there. I'm the minister. My daddy was the minister before me and his daddy before him, and I intend for my son to follow in my steps." The scout replied, "Doesn't the Bible say, 'All have sinned,' and sin means 'falling short?'" If your son doesn't use his God-given gift, isn't that 'falling short'?"

I know that the scout was saying that we should use whatever gifts God has given us, but when the Bible speaks of falling short, it doesn't mean failing to use our sporting talents (as much as Hollywood would like us to think it does). It means falling short of the righteous requirements of the Law of a Holy God.

In 1939, Sue and I were invited to join a group at a very exclusive restaurant in Hollywood. As we entered the building, we found ourselves under the Hollywood spotlight. A very tall gentleman, dressed in an impeccable tuxedo, had the unenviable task of looking us over to see if we were dressed tastefully enough to enter the restaurant. To our astonishment one woman was approached and told that her attire was very nice, but her jacket didn't match the skirt, and she would have to leave. The people with her and her husband said, *"But these are our guests from Germany!"* The answer was firm, "I'm sorry. I have been instructed that she will have to leave." The embarrassed party then left the building.

Before you call the American Civil Liberties Union, consider the following thoughts. First, the people who owned the restaurant had the right to set their own standards, high and snooty though they were. The place certainly was packed. It seemed that once people knew the standard, they conformed.

Second, Jesus told a similar and very sobering story about a guest who was ejected from the Kingdom of God because he wasn't dressed correctly (see Matthew 22:8-13). That's Heaven's standard . . . a robe of righteousness weaved with fine linen. If we don't like it, we can choose the alternative. If the Prodigal Son refuses the robe, neither will he get the ring.

Something Smells

A pastor from Oregon once went on an outreach to Africa. After traveling for over two weeks, he put on a clean white jacket. The trouble was, everywhere he went he could smell this horrible stench. He found himself looking sideways at everyone he came across. Even while traveling open-air on the back of a truck, that putrid smell followed him. After commuting 120 miles he put his hand into an inside pocket of his clean white jacket, and found some processed cheese he had put in there while traveling in the plane to Africa, *over two weeks earlier*.

Each of us wear what we think is a clean garment of righteousness. We think the stench of sin comes from everyone else, when the truth is the rotten cheese of the Adamic nature follows each of us. The cheese is tucked into the pocket of the human heart. The Law points to the pocket.

Take the Law out of the gospel and you take the backbone out of your message. The Law upholds the gospel, and it feeds it with nerves. Without it, it is a lifeless message . . . "foolishness" to the hearer, not worthy of a moment of his consideration. The Law is the foundation, the walls, the roof, of the Kingdom of God. Grace is the door. If we leave off the foundation, walls, and roof, the door goes nowhere.

If ever the Law needs to be manifest from the arsenal of Holy Writ, it is now. The enemy is rampant. There is a sense of unholy unity in Hell's purpose. The devil is tying the foxes' tails together. The cunning demons of lust are running in a frenzy through the field of the world and creating great fires of sexual passion, greed, violence, and lawlessness. It is out of control in every area of society. But there is the means to block the fire. It is through the gospel, when it is heralded biblically.

Sweet Insalts

Have you ever tried to witness to someone and found they have shown no interest? The Law can have the effect of *making* them interested. Let me explain why. It has been said that you can lead a horse to water, but you can't make him drink. True, but you *can* put salt on his tongue. The water is the gospel, the Law is the salt.

The Law makes a man thirst for righteousness. As he catches a glimpse of the Law, in its perfect strictness, he suddenly understands that he must be made clean or he will perish. His God-given will to live will work with you as you labor with the Holy Spirit to give light to his darkened heart.

Jesus didn't say, "Come unto me and drink." He said, *"If any man thirst,* let him come unto me and drink." Unregenerate man has no thirst for righteousness until he understands that he *needs* righteousness, that he must face the Law on Judgment Day. The Law creates desire for the water of grace. He who has crawled through the burning and barren desert of the Law most appreciates the cool, clear waters of the gospel of grace. If you have a sinner who will listen to you, take advantage of that opportunity to create thirst with the Law. The day may come when he refuses to hear the Law, and comes under God's wrath, as happened to Israel in Zechariah 7:12.

Sue and I were once sitting in a restaurant waiting for our food. A woman at the next table had her meal served, and immediately proceeded to scatter what she thought was salt over her food. The salt turned out to be sugar. I don't think she appreciated the meal very much.

The Law is the salt which *creates the desire*, and the gospel is the sugar which *satisfies*. If we get them mixed up, we will never appreciate their individual functions.

Imagine if you told a sinner that you had put a

tiny listening device behind his ear when he was sleeping. Now, because of the miracle of modern technology, you could play back not only his every word and deed, but every thought and imagination that had passed through his mind over the last three months. "Impossible," you say. But that is what his conscience has been doing from the moment he knew right from wrong. The Law pushes the replay button.

Or imagine if you are on a freeway in San Francisco just after a massive earthquake, when you are waved down by an officer of the law. He soberly tells you that you need to detour down a narrow street, because they have found ten large cracks in one of the pillars holding up the deck of an overhead freeway. As you look ahead, you can see where they have clearly marked the cracks on the pillar.

What is it that causes you to gratefully take the detour? It's your knowledge of what will happen when that pillar gives way . . . you will be crushed.

As officers of the Law, we are to soberly point out that the Ten Commandments are going to bring swift destruction upon all those traveling on the freeway of sin. Jesus said the judgment of God will grind the sinner "to powder." When something is ground to powder, a thorough job is done. Judgment under the Law will be exhaustive, right down to every idle word, and every thought of every heart. We can convince them to take the gospel detour if they will allow us to clearly point to the cracks in the Law. Those who are convinced will turn, and turn gratefully.

Think of the attitude of the man who is *unwillingly* manipulated down the detour. He is not told of those ten great cracks, and so he is sent in a different direction than his heart desires. He will never appreciate the safety of the detour, nor will he bother to convince others to take its course.

Do Unto Others

Picture trying to tell a man who is blind that he is heading for a cliff, and having him spurn your words of warning. To him, the path is easy and the air is clean and fresh. He can feel the warmth of the sun on his back, and the sound of the birds above. There is no cause for alarm. But if you care for him, you will take him by the hand and lead him to the edge of the cliff. Then drop two or three stones (or ten if necessary) over for him to hear as they hit the jagged rocks, hundreds of feet below. His own common sense will do the rest. If he is sane, he will gladly turn away from danger.

Many who are living in self-righteousness reveal the fact with the ever popular, "I live by the rule, 'Do to others, as you would have them do unto you.'" This is an excellent entrance for the Law. What they are saying is that they strive to "love their neighbor as themselves." But Jesus said the essence of the Law cannot be separated. We are commanded to love God with all our heart, mind, soul, and strength, *and then* to love our neighbor as ourselves (see Matthew 22:39-40). If someone says they love mankind, but they don't love God, they are guilty of breaking the First Commandment. If they say they have loved God as they should, and their neighbor as much as they love themselves, they are breaking the ninth by lying, because the Scriptures say there is none who understands, and none who seek after God. Their own mouth condemns them.

23

Barren Michal

In speaking of the godly in contrast to the wicked, Psalm 1:2 says that they delight in the Law of the Lord, and they meditate on it day and night. The Psalmist is speaking of the man who is blessed, and is referring to the Law of Moses, which he sees as a "valuable thing," as the meaning is in the Hebrew. What an understatement! The Law is without price because it brings the lost human race into *everlasting life in Christ*. It is the pathway that leads to the Savior; it is the *ladder* of the fireman who rescues the child from a burning house; the *rope* thrown to a drowning person. Those who have cried, "Open my eyes, that I may behold wondrous things out of your Law," have seen the Law's function in reaching sinners so they may be saved from the fires of everlasting Hell. They delight in it for what it does. The ladder is no longer merely a "ladder," the rope which was used is no longer *just a rope*. This is why they say with the Psalmist, "O how I love your Law! it is my meditation all the day" (Psalm 119:97). Those who delight in the Law will dance as David danced, when the ark carried that precious Law into Jerusalem. Those who seek to save the lost, but fail to see that the Law is worthy of delight, may end up like David's wife, Michal.

Son of a Harlot

Jephthah was the son of a harlot, and therefore he had no inheritance in his father's house. The man didn't think about the future. He made a rash vow to God, and therefore cut off his own seed (see Judges 11:30-39). His life is typical of those within the Harlot church.

However, the saved soul lays his hand upon his mouth. He fears the Commandment. He is slow to speak and swift to hear. He meditates on the Law "day and night." That means he ponders over the Law, studies it, and speaks of it. He is "well pleased" with the Law. The word "day" means from sunrise to sunset, and the word "night" not only denotes in the night season, but also in times of adversity . . . in the dark hours of tribulation. In his ignorance, he once thought that the Law stood for bondage and legalism. Now he knows that the Law is the expression of God's character. It stands for justice, truth, and holiness. It epitomizes all that is right and good.

Psalm 19:7 tells us that the Law is perfect, that it converts the soul, makes wise the simple, and we are told further that it was not made for a "righteous man, but for sinners" (1 Timothy 1:9). Modern translators (except the NKJV), not understanding the purpose of the Law, saw no need to keep the Hebrew word *shuwb* as "convert." Instead, they chose other renderings such as "refresh," and "restore," which unfortunately clouds its true function. Bible commentator, Matthew Henry, said of Psalm 19:7: "It is of use to convert the soul, to bring us back to ourselves, to our God, to our duty; for it shows us our sinfulness and misery in our departures from God and the indispensable necessity of our return to Him."

Bible scholars who don't understand the purpose of the Law are, no doubt, mystified as to the meaning of the verse. I certainly was for years, and so I made no objection to the fact that the word "Law" was interpreted by modern versions as the "Word of God" in many places of the Bible. Yet, the Hebrew for Law is again *torah*, referring to the Decalogue or The Pentateuch, the five Books of Moses, the backbone of which is the Ten Commandments.

The dictionary trace of the word is *yaw-raw* meaning, "to point out (as if by aiming the finger), to teach, inform, instruct." How perfectly that describes the "schoolmaster" who leads us to Christ. It was God's finger which "pointed out" the Law to Moses, and now it is the ten fingers of the Law which point out the sin in man's heart. The Law to the sinner is God's finger written on the walls of his conscience, saying, "You are weighed in the balance and found wanting." His state becomes clear in his mind. This is why those who come under the sound of the Law for the first time will say things like, "I understand what you are saying," . . . "That makes sense," . . . "I've never heard it put so clearly before."

Psalm 19:7 also gives us a commendation on the Law. It says the Law of the Lord is *perfect*, meaning "without blemish, complete, full, sound, without spot, undefiled." It is interesting to note that the words used are the same expressions used in the New Testament to describe the state of the Christian. The apostle Paul spoke of the Church, the Chaste Virgin, as being "without spot or blemish" (Ephesians 5:27), saying we are "complete" in Him (see Colossians 2:10), having a "sound" mind (see 2 Timothy 1:7).

If I purchase a perfect antique vase, drop it, and then find that it has a small crack on its base, I have "broken" the vase. Its perfection is shattered. This is why Scripture says, "Whosoever shall keep the whole Law, yet offend in one point, the same is guilty of all" (James 2:10). If we break even one small point of the Law, we have shattered its perfection.

As we saw earlier, Scripture tells us that the Commandment is "a lamp, and the Law is light; and reproofs of instruction are the way of life." What better description can we have of the function of the Law of God? It brings the knowledge of sin. It is the light which causes the darkness to flee. If your hand is unclean and you want to be happy with it, keep it in darkness. But if you want to see it in truth, bring it to the light. If a man knows his soul is unclean and he wants to keep it filthy, he keeps it away from the light of the Law, but if he wants to see himself in truth, he brings it to the radiance of the Commandments.

Much of what Jesus taught was either corrections of Pharisaic perversions of the Law, or echoes of Holy Scripture. He told a lawyer that if he satisfied the Law, he would live (see Luke 10:25,28), something totally in line with God's Word . . . "Keep my Commandments, and live" (Proverbs 7:2). Obey the holy Commandments and live. Disobey and perish.

In Psalm 19:7 we are also told that the Law *converts* the soul. The word is a direct reference to the human mind. The function of the Law is to change a person's mind about his or her state before God.

In 1993 a UCLA student told me that he found that his witness to a friend had little impact. He then came across the teaching of the importance of the Law, and so he took him through the Ten Commandments. The next day his friend called and said, "I have been thinking about what we talked about. You have me in a *Christian checkmate* . . . I've got no way out." He cowered under the ten stones of the Commandments he had so evidently violated. He was "shut up" under the Law, and came to the Savior a short time later.

I am often asked if I would lead a sinner in a prayer of repentance. This can be answered by asking the question, *Why did Jesus appear to Thomas on the eighth day?* This is dealt with in depth in our publication, *The Undertaker's Nightmare*.

Time Will Make This Plain

A great preacher of the past warned, "Evermore the Law *must* prepare the way for the gospel. To overlook this in instructing souls, is almost certain to result in false hope, the introduction of a false standard of Christian experience, and to fill the Church with false converts . . . time will make this plain."

Look at these wise words from Charles Spurgeon (we looked at part of this quote in an earlier chapter), "Lower the Law and you dim the light by which man perceives his guilt; this is a very serious loss to the sinner rather than a gain; for it lessens the likelihood of his conviction and conversion. I say you have deprived the gospel of its ablest auxiliary (its most powerful weapon) when you have set aside the Law. You have taken away from it the schoolmaster that is to bring men to Christ . . . *They will never accept grace till they tremble before a just and holy Law*. Therefore the Law serves a most necessary purpose, and it must not be removed from its place."

We have moved so far from Scripture, statements like this, seem foreign to us.

Martin Luther gives the prioritized order of gospel proclamation: "The first duty of the gospel preacher is to declare God's Law and show the nature of sin."

Signs and Wonders

Genuine words of knowledge and evident healings are biblical and very desirable. Who of us doesn't want to see a cancer sufferer healed in answer to prayer? Such demonstrations of the power of God can open a person's eyes to His concern for them as individuals. An undeniable miracle can stir the deepest emotions, but the Law converts the soul, brings the knowledge of sin, and acts as a schoolmaster to bring sinners to Christ. Simon the Magician's false conversion came as a result of evident miracles at the hands of the Apostles. But he was still in the "bond of lawlessness" (Acts 8:23). Salvation doesn't occur as a result of a decision, a conviction, or an acknowledgment, but as the outcome of repentance towards God (the One offended), and faith toward our Lord Jesus Christ (the only Name under Heaven whereby we must be saved).

Matthew Henry so rightly said, "Those that would know sin must get the knowledge of the Law in its strictness, extent, and spiritual nature." Commenting on the function of the Law in its capacity to bring the knowledge of sin, he said, "Of this excellent use is the Law; it converts the soul, opens the eyes, prepares the way of the Lord in the desert, rends the rocks, levels the mountains, makes a people prepared for the Lord."

Jesus told His disciples to go to the "highways and hedges," and to compel them to come in (see Luke 14:23). There are many who walk the highways of sin. Their course is one of willful rebellion to the light God has given. They are on the road to damnation, and the Law must be used as a signpost to warn them of their terrible destination. There are others who hide amidst the hedges of self-righteousness. They have a faith in God, but not a saving faith. They have a morality, but their conscience is not purged from dead works to serve the living God (see Hebrews 9:14). They haven't applied the blood because they haven't been plagued by the Law of God. The Law must be used to flush them out of their false sense of security.

Each year, according to *World Christian Encyclopedia*, approximately $17,600 *million* is spent on evangelism. One would think with such a budget we could do the job. Also, each year 50 million people die. According to the study, we can be consoled that of the 50 million who passed into eternity, 15 million professed faith in Jesus Christ. However, God only knows how many of those 15 million were still in the darkness, enshrouded by the mantle of the Harlot, and how many came under the sound of Law before grace and found a place of "repentance unto life."

24

As Sure as Hell

The key to putting the Harlot out of business is for sinners to betroth their hearts to another through genuine conversion. The way to do this is to show them His passionate, undying love, demonstrated in the Cross of Calvary. How does one best preach Christ crucified? By showing how *unworthy* we are of such love.

The gospel is the story of the King giving his life for the criminal. It is the tale of the Handsome Prince of Peace, giving the kiss of life to the sleeping Snow White Bride of Christ. A story of such great love must never be trifled with. It must be presented to a dying world with sobriety and "great plainness of speech," least they misunderstand and reject our report. Sin, in all its blackness must be made bare, so that the beam of the light of the glorious gospel shines in all its brilliance.

Giving God His Dues

For those Christians who are still not convinced, let's look at the case of the Law from another angle. If we ignore the Law, we will find that Jews won't receive what we have to say. There are literally millions of Jews who have about the same amount of faith in the New Testament that you and I have for the *Book of Mormon*. If you preach and make the point of moral reference the New Testament, rather than pointing as Jesus did to the Ten Commandments, then you can be sure that most of what you say will be totally disregarded by a Jew. If we want to reach God's people with the gospel, we should therefore hang all our New Testament theology on the Law and the prophets. Paul did: "And to the Jews I became as a Jew, that I might win Jews; to those who are under the Law, as under the Law, that I might win those who are under the Law; to those who are without Law, as without Law, (not being without Law toward God, but under law toward Christ), that I might win those who are without Law" (1 Corinthians 9:20-21).

Gnat Soup

The State of Israel needs God's Law to show them the state of Israel. In an article written by a

244

prominent Jewish rabbi, he spoke of something called "nullification." In it he said, "Should something non-kosher fall into a pot of hot kosher soup, one need not throw out the soup if the ration of kosher to non-kosher is more than sixty to one. The forbidden fragment becomes nullified in the larger vat" (*Jerusalem Post*, February, 1993).

Nothing has changed. They strain at the vat and swallow the camel. They are concerned about what falls into a vat, yet look at how they nullify the Law: In the same article, the rabbi said, "The whole purpose of the Commandments is to purify and unite humanity." How can the mirror cleanse the beholder? If it was read in truth, it would show them their uncleanness, and send them fleeing in repentance to Him whose hands they pierced. Their tradition has made void the Commandments of God.

We may smile at such trifles as vat-straining. As the Church of God, we take great pains to keep free from the rituals that so bind the modern Jew and the traditional church. We may not wear robes, recite long prayers and carry candles, but we have become enrobed in our method of evangelism. We carry the candles of decision cards, emotional altar calls, and follow up. To leave a new convert solely in God's hands is anathema.

The blind Pharisees laid aside the Commandment of God that they might hold onto their tradition . . . "the washing of pots and cups" (Mark 7:7-8). The modern Church has done the same. We have laid aside the Commandment of God, and because our method of evangelism is *traditional* rather than *biblical*, our converts are pots and cups which are clean on the outside but filthy on the inside. Many are strangers to regenerative cleansing by the Holy Spirit.

Confirmed in Their Error

I was talking to an elderly lady at an airport once, when she remarked that she had a touch of arthritis. Then she said, "I'm not old, *but I've sure as Hell been young a long time,"* and laughed. I said, "It's funny how we use sayings like that . . . "sure as Hell." She laughed some more. Then I said, "When you know it exists, you stop laughing." She stopped laughing, and took a tract. Surprisingly, 62% of Americans believe in a literal Hell, *but they flatter themselves, like most of the unregenerate, with the thought that they will not go there*. As far as they are concerned, Heaven can't wait to have their holy presence. Their proud presumption exhibits their lamentable ignorance.

Many preach a gospel that makes mention of Hell, sin and Heaven, but because they fail to use the Law to show that sin is "exceedingly sinful" (see Romans 7:13), it just confirms the sinner in his error. He lacks knowledge of what sin is, and therefore he thinks he is on his way to Heaven. When the preacher says the customary, "God wants you to have the assurance of Heaven," he merely gives his life to Christ and confirms what he believed all along . . . that he *deserves* Heaven. His ignorance robs him of understanding the mercy extended in the Cross. Calvary was Heaven freely given, when Hell was all that was deserved. He then lacks appreciation, and therefore gratitude for the mercy of God, and gratitude is the prime motivation for evangelism. This is why the modern "convert" lacks zeal for the lost. He neither knows what he (supposedly) has been saved from, or saved for.

Then there are preachers, who because they lack the weapon of the Law, revert to a sermon on Hell, giving gruesome graphic details. Their words have much heat but no light, and without the light of the Law will produce a dread without repentance. The decisions are *dreadful*, rather than *tearful*, because there is still no knowledge of sin. The convert thinks God is harsh and unjust, and he comes only to escape the fires of Hell. But the Law-fleeing convert comes with the *understanding* that he deserves Hell, yet God has given him Heaven. He knows that if the Ten Commandments judged him on that Day, he would be condemned. He realizes that if his unclean thoughts, his deeds of darkness, and the sins of his youth were brought out as evidence of his guilt, he would be cast into Hell. What's more, justice would be done. Rather, God has given him mercy, and instead of death, he has been given life. Instead of eternal suffering, he will have eternal pleasure. He falls prostrate in the bloodied soil of Calvary's Cross, horrified at the cost of his redemption. He sees Jesus Christ evidently set forth and crucified to satisfy the demands of the Law. His spirit is broken by such love. He burns with gratitude for such an unspeakable gift, living for God's will and honor.

Plane Understanding

Let's use an analogy to see how we can stop the terrible fatalities we looked at in a previous chapter (this is further developed from a similar analogy in my book, *Hell's Best Kept Secret*, published by Whitaker House).

There was once a man seated on a plane. As

he enjoyed the flight, ate his meal and watched the movie, he suddenly heard, "This is your captain speaking; I have an announcement to make. As this plane is about to crash, you are going to have to jump. We would therefore appreciate it if you would put your parachutes on."

He takes one look out of the window at the 25,000 foot drop, and immediately puts the parachute on. Then he looks at the man next to him, and to his horror, sees that he is still looking at the movie. He nudges him and says, *"Didn't you hear the captain; put the parachute on!"*

But the gentleman casually says, "I don't think the captain really means it . . . besides, I'm quite happy as I am thanks."

The man with the parachute so wants him to be saved, he does a strange thing. He says, "Please put on the parachute . . . *it will make your flight much better.*"

Can you see that this gives the man a *wrong motive* for putting the parachute on? If he puts it on to improve his flight, as soon as it gets bumpy, he will take it off. Instead, he should tell him about the jump. He should show him the 25,000 foot drop and remind him of the law of gravity. If he did that, and the man saw his terrible danger, he would immediately (and gratefully) put the parachute on . . . *and as long as he knew he was going to have to jump, there would be no way anyone could get him to take that parachute off his back.* Think about it. As long as that man knows he's going to have to jump out of the plane and face the consequences of breaking the law of gravity, there is *no way* you are going to get the parachute off his back, *because his life depends on it!*

Can you see that his motive, *his reason for putting it on,* is that which determines whether or not he keeps the parachute on?

As we look around humanity, we see that multitudes of "passengers" are enjoying the flight. They are enjoying the pleasures of sin for a season. But modern evangelism says (in zeal without knowledge), "Did you hear the command from the Captain of our Salvation, 'Put on the Lord Jesus Christ?' He will give you love, joy, peace, fulfillment, and lasting happiness. He will fill the God-shaped vacuum in your heart, will help your alcohol problem and your drug problem. He will take away your loneliness and also heal your marriage problem . . . just give your heart to Jesus." In other words, Jesus will improve your flight.

The message gives a *wrong motive* for sinners to come to the Savior. Instead, we must take courage and tell them about the jump; that it is appointed for them once to die, then after this, the Judgment (see Hebrews 9:27). We need to open up the Commandments and show them they must face the fearful consequences of breaking the Law of God (see Romans 2:12; James 2:12). Then let that knowledge (with the help of the Holy Spirit) convince them they need the Savior, in the same way the law of gravity convinced the passenger he needed a parachute. When they respond to the gospel and put on the Lord Jesus Christ to be saved from the wrath to come (like the man who put the parachute on to be saved from the jump would never forsake it because his life depended on it), so these converts will never "backslide." *This is because their eternal salvation depends on their relationship with Jesus*. Their knowledge of the consequences of breaking the Law of God causes them to cling *for their very lives* to the Savior.

As you enter the customs and immigration area of Los Angeles airport, you will see a notice which states, "Declare it! Dump it! Or face a $25,000 fine." Under the notice sits a large box with a slot in it. Travelers have a decision to make. Either they declare their illegal goods and pay customs, dump it in the box, or risk a massive fine.

There lies the simplicity of the gospel message. Sinners have a choice. They must confess and forsake their sins in Christ, or face the wrath of God's Law.

Double Honor

I often talk to Christians who understand the imperative nature of preaching the Law before grace, but they are frustrated because they are surrounded by others who carry on evangelizing with modern methods. Often, it's the pastor who fills the altar each week, without the use of the Law. This is what you should do. Be careful that you don't despise the man to whom God tells you to give "double honor" (see 1 Timothy 5:17). If you decide to give him a copy of this book, make sure you don't give him the impression you are saying, "Pastor, you need to read this!" Instead, say something like, "Pastor, I would value your opinion of this book." Then pray.

Those who use modern methods don't realize that their ears are closed because they are set in their tradition. They don't understand that they are actually damaging the cause they are trying to promote. These brethren are like the man who was brought to Jesus who was deaf and had an impediment in his speech. We must do what Jesus did. He looked towards Heaven and sighed (see Mark 7:34). It is prayer that opens ears. When the man's ears were opened, then he spoke plainly. It is when the Church's ears are opened by God to the importance of using the Law to bring the knowledge of sin, that she will speak clearly, and sinners will understand and be saved.

25

Getting a Handle On It

Earlier in this book, we were consoled with the fact that even though there was a massive fall away rate with the proclamation of the modern gospel, there were those who did actually enter the Kingdom of God. There were the 14,337 we looked at, at the beginning of this book, who remained in fellowship despite the fact that most fell away.

It was a respected preacher who warned that if the Ten Commandments were dropped from the gospel proclamation, the result would almost certainly be to "fill the Church with false converts." What specifically did he mean by a "false" convert?

The Bible has much to say on the subject. The apostle Paul speaks twice of "false brethren" (see 2 Corinthians 11:26; Galatians 2:4), of those who had risen within the Church to the point of being false apostles (see 2 Corinthians 11:13), and also of false teachers (see 2 Peter 2:1).

In Matthew 7:21-23, we see perhaps the most sobering verses in the Bible: "Not everyone who says to Me, 'Lord, Lord,' shall enter the Kingdom of Heaven, but he who does the will of My Father in Heaven. Many will say to Me in that day, 'Lord, Lord, have we not prophesied in Your name, cast out demons in Your name, and done many wonders in Your name?' And then I will declare to them, 'I never knew you; depart from Me, you who practice lawlessness!'"

Here we have *many* who will be cast from the gates of Heaven into Hell. But look closely at the wording. These people will be those who called Jesus "Lord." That means they *said* He was the supreme authority in their lives. They *professed* that He was the One to whom they gave complete allegiance . . . that they loved Him with all their heart, mind, soul, and strength. By calling Jesus "Lord," they said they acknowledged Him in all their ways. Every thought, every deed, and every word came in the light of His Lordship.

But more than that, they had works which attested to their apparent redemption. They prophesied in His name, they cast out demons in

His name and they did many wonderful works in His name. Yet, Jesus will say to them, "I never knew you; depart from me . . . " He didn't know them because they were "workers of iniquity" (KJV). The word "iniquity" is *anomia,* which means "illegality . . . violation of Law . . . transgression of the Law."

Jesus never knew them *at any time,* as it says in the original tongue. These were not ones who were saved, then turned their backs on the holy commandment. He said He *never* knew them: "Whoever sins, has not seen Him, *neither known Him*" (1 John 3:6, italics added). They were false conversions, who said they loved the Lord Jesus Christ, but in specific works denied Him. They named the name of Christ, but never departed from their lawless deeds. They were workers of iniquity and at the same time they said they were Christians. They expected to go to Heaven, called Jesus "Lord," prophesied in His name, cast out demons in His name and did many wonderful (Greek: *dunamis*) works in His name.

Then, following those verses, Jesus told a story of two men, one built his house on rock, the other on sand. The common interpretation of this story is that the wise man is the believer, and the foolish man is a type of the ungodly. However, on closer examination, the man who built his house on sand *cannot* be an unbeliever. When the Scriptures say he that "hears" these sayings and doesn't do them, it uses the same word it uses for the wise man, *akouo,* which means "to understand." So Scripture is not speaking about those who are in ignorance, but of those who *understand* the sayings of Jesus. The unsaved are "dead" spiritually (see Ephesians 2:1), in the lusts of their ignorance. We know from God's Word that the ungodly man is in darkness, he *cannot* see (see John 3:3), his understanding is darkened, being alienated from the life of God through the ignorance that is in him, because of the blindness of his heart (see Ephesians 4:18). The natural man doesn't receive the things of the Spirit of God, for they are foolishness to him; *nor can he know them,* because they are spiritually discerned (see 1 Corinthians 2:14). As we have seen previously, the Bible tells us that there is *none* that understands (see Romans 3:11).

The unsaved don't understand the words of Jesus. Their knowledge is usually limited to "do to others, as you would have them do to you," and "judge not lest you be judged," and even then they have a twisted perception as to what the Scriptures say.

Getting a Handle On It

This parable is rather speaking of the true and the false convert. The false convert sits among true believers and hears Jesus' commands to, "Go into all the world and preach the gospel to every creature," to "preach the word, be instant in season and out of season," to "teach all nations," to "let your light shine," and be His "witnesses." Yet, he does not obey the great commission. His feet are not shod with the preparation of the gospel of peace.

Jesus then gave us the reason that so many will be excluded from the Kingdom of God. These people heard and understood His teachings, *but never obeyed them*. They were not His sheep. They never heard His voice, because He said He *never* knew them. They didn't do the will of His Father who is in Heaven.

Remember, he who says, "I know Him," and does not keep His commandments, is a liar, and the truth is not in him. If we are born of His Spirit, we will delight to do His will. Jesus said, "He that has My commandments, and keeps them, he it is who loves Me." Even though we are in "weakness, fear and much trembling," we will say "Here I am Lord, send me." The door of salvation hinges upon obedience. The Christian isn't saved because he's obedient. He is obedient *because* he is saved. He will bring forth fruit to confirm his salvation: "Even so, *every* good tree bears good fruit" (Matthew 7:17, italics added). The "fruit of the Spirit" is evidence of the work of the Holy Spirit in the life of the believer.

Jesus is the Door, and those who come to Him must get a handle on the fact that they are to obey His Word, or the door will never open. They will find themselves thrust out of the Kingdom of God. They have the choice of "sin unto death," or of "obedience unto righteousness" (Romans 6:16). James warned that the mantle of deception and disobedience go hand in hand, saying to be "doers of the word, and not hearers only, *deceiving your own selves*" (James 1:22, italics added).

The Error of Presumption

A pastor attended a funeral of an acquaintance of someone in his congregation. He was horrified to hear the minister say that the deceased had given his heart to Jesus at eight years of age, and therefore everyone at the funeral would see him again. His words may have been consoling to the hearers, but it was a great error to presume that all who were at the funeral were saved. God only knows if the man who died was a Christian. The fact that he was shot to death while at a topless bar cuts back the odds somewhat. He certainly wasn't there to witness for the faith.

Sinners can only be sure they are "elect according to the foreknowledge of God," if their heart is brought "into obedience and sprinkling of the blood of Jesus Christ" (1 Peter 1:2). Stay with me, because we will continue these vital thoughts in the next chapter.

26
Foul Fowl

In Mark 4:30, Jesus likened the Kingdom of God to a tree which has "birds" in it. As we have seen earlier, birds in Scripture are often likened to demons (see Mark 4:4,15; Revelation 18:2). The Church of God, this great "planting of the Lord," has, hidden within the branches of its pews, masses of children of the devil. We can't see the two classes of true and false clearly at the moment. But at the Great Judgment when Jesus separates the "sheep from the goats," we will see the final division of those who are His sheep and those He calls goats, the children of the devil. On that day, we shall "discern between the righteous and the wicked, between him that serves God and him that serves him not" (Malachi 3:18).

Judas typified the false convert. God only

knows if he was truly saved, but it seems to me that he never knew Jesus in the intimate fellowship of being a child of the Living God. He had no idea who Jesus was, revealed in the fact of his selling of the Son of God for thirty pieces of silver. This was the ultimate treasure of the very source of life itself manifest in the flesh; all the riches of this world are but dung in comparison. His covetous heart betrayed itself, when he complained that good money had been wasted in an extravagant act of worship, when a sinful woman broke an alabaster box of ointment and anointed Jesus. As far as he was concerned, Jesus wasn't worthy of such worship. Judas did everything right outwardly. He maintained he cared for the poor, no doubt sung the hymns with the other disciples, healed the sick, attended the fellowship, and looked after the finances, but he was a "worker of iniquity." He broke the 8th Commandment. The Bible says he was a thief (see John 12:6).

The Great Pretender

Notice in the parable of the sheep and goats, that the goats . . . who were sent into everlasting punishment . . . called Jesus "Lord" (see Matthew 25:44). They may have professed faith, but again, in works they denied Him. Then, look at the "evil servant" Jesus spoke of in Matthew 24:45-51, who said, "My Lord delays His coming." This evil servant is called a "servant," believed in the Second Coming and called Jesus "Lord." Yet he was cast in with the hypocrites, where there shall be "weeping and gnashing of teeth." The fact is, he was a hypocrite, and therefore was one who merely *pretended* to be a Christian. He insinuated that he belonged to the Lord, but his life didn't match his claims.

Jesus then immediately spoke of the five wise virgins (genuine converts) and the five foolish virgins (false converts). The false cried out, "Lord, Lord, open to us. But he answered and said, Verily I say unto you, I know you not" (Matthew 25:11-12). Notice that the five foolish virgins also called Jesus "Lord," and again we are told He said, "*I know you not*." There was no intimate fellowship with the Savior. In contrast, the wise virgins had made themselves ready for His coming.

Following these words, Jesus related the Parable of the Talents. In Matthew 25:24, we see that the wicked and slothful servant also called Jesus his "Lord," and then the Scriptures reveal the man's mistake: "Then he that had received the one talent came and said, 'Lord, I knew you to be a hard man, reaping where you have not sown, and gathering where you have not scattered seed.'" His great mistake was that he didn't know Jesus. He *said* he did, but he didn't. This is clearly evidenced by his lack of "things that accompany salvation."

What's the Difference?

With these thoughts in mind, we as witnesses of the gospel must see that it is not enough to get sinners to "name the name of Christ." It doesn't matter if they are brought into fellowship with believers, how radical their change of lifestyle, how many godly activities they get involved in, how many signs and wonders follow their preaching, how many demons they cast out, *because if they continue to walk in lawlessness, they are proving to be false converts.*

The difference between the true and false conversion is seen in that the good soil convert *hears the word* and he *understands* what was being preached (see Matthew 13:23). The Greek word for "heard" means that he grasped the issues, and "understand" is *suniemi*, which means "to mentally comprehend." This is why John Wycliffe maintained, "The highest service to which a man may

attain on earth, is to preach the Law of God."
Why? Because it brings the "knowledge of sin"
(Romans 3:20); it is a "schoolmaster" that teaches
(see Galatians 3:24). It causes light to come to the
darkened unregenerate mind, because, the Commandment is a lamp; and the Law is light; and
reproofs of instruction are the way of life.

The Law brings *understanding* to those who
are in darkness, *the determining factor in "good
soil" hearers:* "Understanding is a wellspring of
life unto him that has it" (Proverbs 1:22).
Remember that Jesus said those who teach the
Law would be called great in God's Kingdom (see
Matthew 5:19), as we have seen earlier. This is
why Philip the evangelist saw fit to ask the
Ethiopian eunuch, "Do you *understand* what you
read?" (italics added). Do you remember the
question Jesus asked the "certain lawyer" in Luke
10:26? He said, "What is written in the Law?
What is your reading of it?" Why did he ask him
how he interpreted the Law? The answer is plain
. . . the man's salvation depended upon his
understanding. If there was no knowledge of sin,
then there would be no repentance, and if there
was no repentance, the man would perish.

Study Nehemiah 8:1-10, and notice how there
was a necessity for understanding when it came to

hearing the Law, then look at the effect on those who understood: "For all the people wept, when they heard the words of the Law." The objective was one of causing the people to understand the Law, by reading it "distinctly" and giving "the sense" of it. The effect was one of contrition.

Matthew 13:19 says that when someone hears the word of the Kingdom and does not understand it, then the wicked one comes and snatches away what was sown in his heart. The hearer, because he doesn't understand, *allows* the devil to take the seed. He does not *value* the seed of the gospel. The Greek word for "understanding" means "put it together." The Jews "put it together" on the Day of Pentecost. They had gathered to celebrate the giving of the Law, so they no doubt had thorough understanding of the Commandments. The Scriptures tell us they were "devout" Jews. The word is *eulabes* and means "taking well (carefully)." The Law was a schoolmaster to bring three thousand to Christ on that day.

When a man feels the heat of the flames, and breathes in the choking smoke, something in his understanding kicks in. It is his understanding that makes him take hold of the fireman's hand.

The same word *eulabes,* is used to describe Simeon, who so readily accepted the Messiah in

Luke 2:25. He had an understanding of who Jesus was. *To leave a sinner without the knowledge of sin which the Law gives, is to invite the devil to snatch away the seed of the gospel.* It leaves him without the understanding, which only the schoolmaster can bring. Its purpose is to cause the knowledge of sin, and thus prepare the heart to *appreciate* grace.

As we saw in the opening chapter of this book, when Paul spoke about Law and grace in Romans 5:20, he said that the Law entered, that "the offense might abound. But where sin abounded, grace did much more abound." If we want the sinner to see grace as he should, the way to do so is to have the Law enter and make the transgression increase. The Law magnifies sin, grace magnifies God. The greater the sinner sees his offense against the Law, the more pronounced grace will be to him, and therefore he will value the sin offering.

27

Research on Adultery

While speaking to his congregation, a pastor noticed that a young girl in the front row sat wide-eyed. She seemed to be hanging on every word he said. This greatly encouraged him. He had the thought that if he could hold the attention of a small child, how much more would the adults be absorbing what he had to say!

After the sermon he approached the girl and said, "Young lady, I noticed you were listening carefully to every word I said." She looked at him and said, "Do you realize you said the word *the* 242 times?"

Sometimes people hear what we have to say, but they miss the message we are trying to get across. The arrow may be fired with great power, but it is a vain exercise if it misses the target of the hearer's understanding. If we study Proverbs 9:1-6, we see what seems to be the true Church personified, calling out to the ungodly that she has understanding which leads to life. The Church has knowledge and wisdom which will cause sinners to "forsake the foolish" *that they might live*. If they can understand their state before God and their need of His forgiveness, they can secure their eternal destiny.

The Right Number

It was a Friday afternoon. The phone rang, so I picked it up and heard, "Is that Direct Imports?" I said it wasn't and asked what number the man wanted. He gave our number so I said, "Well, that is our number, but before you go . . . *make sure you read your Bible*." He went quiet, then said, "Why's that?" I said so that he could find how to secure his eternal destiny and added, " . . . and there's nothing more important than that, is there?" He said, "Yi, yi, yi . . . *I'd better sit down for this!*" I asked, "Are you Jewish?" When he said he was, I told him that I was also Jewish and remarked, "Remember, you've got to face the Ten Commandments on Judgment Day." His reply was interesting: "I have done research, specifically on the adultery one, and I've come to the conclusion that you can fool around with a woman, as long as she's not married." I said, "If you as much as *look* with lust, the Bible says that you commit adultery in your heart. Have you ever told a lie?" He had. I asked if he had stolen, he had. So I gently told him that he was, by his own admission, a lying thief and that's why he needed the Savior Jesus Christ, to save him from God's anger. Then I told him to read his Bible and seek God for the salvation of his soul. I also invited him to call my number any time if he wanted to talk in the future. His voice sounded quite depressed as he said, "Thank you very much for talking to me." I think I ruined his weekend.

In Romans, chapter 10, Paul cited the error of the Jews of his day as being a lack of understanding, which left them ignorant of God's righteousness. They forsook the Law and went about to establish their own standard of righteousness, not having submitted themselves to the righteousness of God. They had "done research" and come to their own conclusions. Like Pontius Pilate, the unregenerate wash their hands in the water of human virtue. The Law turns the water to blood. Their sinful hands become as scarlet, until they are driven by the schoolmaster to the cleansing power of the gospel, and made as white as snow.

Then the apostle Paul said that Christ is the end of the Law *for righteousness* to every one that believes (see Romans 10:1-3). The whole context of this passage has to do with the Law. These Jews were living in self-righteousness, and the reason for this was a lack of knowledge of the Law of God. They misunderstood that the Law required truth in the inward parts, that it was spiritual, and so they were deceived into thinking they could establish their own righteousness.

Lord and Savior

I once gave one of our I.Q. card tracts to a smiley young man in his early twenties. The card gives a simple and fascinating intelligence test then asks another six questions as an "intelligence test," about God, sin, etc. His first hesitation came when he didn't know whether or not God would punish sin. I asked him what God's reaction should be if his sister was raped and murdered. Should He smile or be angry? He said, "Be angry." Then he agreed that it was right that God should punish sin. Next he said that you "avoid Hell by living a good life." This man had no understanding of salvation, so we went through the Commandments. Then I asked him where he would go if he died that day. He confidently said,

"Heaven." I asked why, and he said, "I have accepted Jesus Christ as Lord and Savior."

He then confided in me that he wasn't reading the Bible, and the reason he began in the first place was because he thought it would be an "interesting" book. He told me how a Christian once asked him where he would go if he died. His answer was, "I don't know what God's standards are." The Christian then said, "That doesn't matter. All that really matters is, *have you accepted Jesus Christ as Lord and Savior?"*

Here we have a young man who has no understanding whatsoever about grace (that salvation is a free gift), nor does he have any knowledge of sin. He is unwittingly seeking salvation by works. His understanding of God is idolatrous in that he doesn't even know if He has the backbone to punish sin. Neither does he bother to read the Bible, and therefore should not claim that he is a disciple and Jesus is his Lord (see John 8:31-32), the sovereign master in his life. *Yet, he was given assurance that he is saved because he has "accepted Jesus Christ as Lord and Savior."* How then did he repent if he had no knowledge of sin? How could he work *out* his salvation with fear and trembling, if he is working *for* it? How could he live in holiness when he had no idea of what holiness was? God only knows how many are in the same predicament as this poor man because of modern evangelism's zeal without knowledge.

As a Christian I am sure you can appreciate how wrong it would be to withhold grace from someone who is trembling under the Law. But few see how equally mistaken it is to give a person, who has no knowledge of sin, grace without Law. To do so is to place the satin pillow of the gospel under the head of a sleeping sinner. What he needs is the thunder and lightning of Sinai to awaken him and give him the light of understanding within his darkened mind.

To minister grace without Law is to give him medicine when he doesn't believe he is sick. We shouldn't then be surprised if he pours it down the drain when we are not looking.

The Hands of a Guru

A zealous Christian told me that he felt frustrated. He witnessed to a woman, using the Law, then he told her "about Jesus," and yet she still seemed unconcerned about her salvation. I explained that premature preaching of the Cross to an impenitent sinner may rob the Law of its power. It is to acquit the criminal before he sees the sobering repercussions of his unlawful life-style. Think of the Philippian jailer's words, "Sirs, what must I do to be saved?" (Acts 16:30). Had he been given grace already, he would not have had to ask how to be saved. This was also the case with the Jews on the Day of Pentecost when they asked, "Men and brethren, what shall we do?" (Acts 2:37). Jesus withheld grace from the lawyer who tempted him (see Luke 10:25), and from the rich young ruler (see Luke 18:18). Paul did not reason with Felix about "righteousness, temperance, judgment, *grace, and mercy*." Felix might not have trembled if he had been told that God was love, and that He was good, kind, and merciful. Love withholds grace with the view of seeing biblical repentance.

A well-known author told an old story about a man who wanted to find God. He sought out an Indian guru, who took him to a river. After wading into the water, the man allowed the gentle-speaking guru to lower him beneath its surface, thinking that he was being baptized. However, he surprisingly felt the guru's hands tense, and hold him under the water. He struggled as a sense of panic began to grip his mind. No matter how hard he battled, the strong arms of the old man held him under the cold water. Adrenalin pumped through his terrified body. *He must get air or die!*

Suddenly, the man let go and he burst through the water's surface. *He couldn't understand why the guru would do such a senseless thing to him.* The old man raised his hand to calm him, and said, "When you *yearn* for God as much as you craved for oxygen, *then* you will find Him."

The author who told the old story, then likened it to how a *Christian* should desire God. By an act of our will, the godly person determines to desire God (see Psalm 27:4). The *ungodly* however, have no desire for God (see Romans 3:11). This is where the Law gives a helping hand. The strong arm of the Law holds the sinner beneath the waters of iniquity. He suddenly realizes that he must break free from its deadly grip, or he will perish.

Remember the words of Faithful and Christian in, *Pilgrim's Progress* as they spoke of the function of the Law in their lives: *"Then he did to us a favor,"* answered Christian. Faithful then shows how the Law grips us: *"Aye. Albeit, he did it none too gently."* Its purpose isn't to take our life from us, but to make us crave the oxygen of God's mercy in Christ.

28
The Well-Oiled Gate

If you witness regularly, you will know how many in contemporary America think they are good people. This is the fruit of a nation that has forsaken God's Law. The Law is "good," and when there is no knowledge of the Law, "good" becomes subjective. This was the case with the rich young ruler's "Good Master, what good thing shall I do that I may have eternal life?" (Matthew 19:16). Jesus reproved his misuse of the word "good." He was one who used the word without knowledge of its true meaning.

Sinners often say similar things. An athlete may say that "the good Man upstairs" helped him win a race. Or they seek to justify their sin by saying, "You're a good person; tell me . . . " This is why I find it frustrating when I do a good deed for someone who doesn't know that I am a

Christian. If I help push a car, etc., I don't want them to think, "I knew there were still good people. That restores my faith in human nature." Often, the more "good" people the world can find, the more they will try to justify their own goodness, and reject God's mercy. Like the rich young ruler, they need to be enlightened as to what *good* is. The way to do this is to follow the example of Jesus and decimate the fig leaves of self-righteousness with the Ten Cannons of God's Law.

A famous Rogers and Hammerstein musical contained the words, "Somewhere in my childhood, I must have done something good." The young lady who was singing the song had fallen in love and was brimming with happiness. It was her way of saying that God was rewarding her with the blessing of true love, because she merited it. While God does reward good and evil, her words exemplify the world's erroneous philosophy. Any good that comes our way doesn't solely come to us because *we* have done something good, but because *God* is good. Until we understand that "there is none good, no not one," we will expect blessings because we think we are good and therefore deserve them. When life deals us suffering, we become angry at God because we think God *owes* us happiness.

The Well-Oiled Gate

The Law not only gives us understanding of the grace of the Cross, but of the grace of life itself . . . that He has not dealt with us according to our iniquities. The only thing God owes us is wrath.

A man in London airport decided to purchase some English "butter" cookies. He opened the small tin, took one out then placed the tin at his feet. After waiting for his flight for some time, a middle-aged woman smiled politely and sat next to him. To his astonishment, without a word of permission she reached down, took a cookie out of the tin and ate it. He couldn't believe what this complete stranger had just done. Suspecting that it may be a local custom, he smiled at her and took one himself. A few minutes later, she took another one. He smiled awkwardly and took a second cookie himself. She then took a third. *Who did this woman think she was!* Then she took the very last cookie, looked at him, broke it in half and offered it to him. *The audacity of the woman!* Different words such as "impudent, rude, brazen and presumptuous" flashed through his mind.

As he was about to express his thoughts, he bent down and saw that his identical tin of cookies was still at his feet. In an instant, he realized that *he* had been the brazen, rude, impudent, and presumptuous person. *He had been eating the cookies of a complete stranger!* He also realized how her response to his actions had in truth been very gracious.

Unregenerate humanity judges God as being the guilty party for the sufferings of humanity. As far as they are concerned, He is unjust. But the Law of God gives us sudden light to our misconception. It shows us who is eating whose cookies. *We* are the ones that are in transgression. It dawns on us that we are *more* than brazenly impudent in our accusations. We are guilty criminals standing before an unspeakably holy and gracious Judge, accusing Him of transgression. In the light of God's holiness, it is hard to understand why He continues to let a sinful humanity such as us even draw another breath.

Three Repercussions

Notice that Paul, in Acts 13:15-16, *after the Law had been read,* preached Christ crucified to those Jews "who feared God." The result of this harmony of Law and grace was that many of the Jews and religious proselytes followed Paul and Barnabas, who speaking to them, persuaded them to continue in the grace of God.

If the Law is not understood, it has at least three solemn repercussions:

1. The convert won't appreciate the Law's potential evangelistically. Therefore any soul who makes a commitment from the seed of his ministry will more than likely be reproduced after his kind.

2. He will have no understanding of the spiritual nature of the Law (that God requires "truth in the inward parts"), so he will continue to live in inward lawlessness.

3. He will never fully comprehend nor appreciate the comfort and blessings of the gospel.

"But," you say, "it is the *Holy Spirit* who convicts of sin, righteousness and judgment . . . it is the *Holy Spirit* who saves sinners." Why then do we bother to preach at all? Why then do the Scriptures say, "How will they hear without a preacher?" Why does the Word say that God has chosen "the foolishness of *preaching* to save them that believe?"

The Holy Spirit is the One who convicts and saves sinners, but He has chosen the foolishness of preaching to save them that believe, and they won't have a faith that leads to salvation if they don't understand. Therefore we must preach what God has ordained us to preach, the "whole counsel of God." That includes the Law, the Cross, the resurrection, faith, and repentance. When Paul summed up the gospel he made very clear reference to the resurrection as being part and parcel of it (see 1 Corinthians 15:3-4). The resurrection to the gospel, is like water to the ocean. If Christ be not risen, then all our labor is in vain.

When the disciples "preached the resurrection" (see Acts 4:2; 17:18), was this a reference to the resurrection of the dead, when all that are in their graves shall hear His voice, or was it specifically speaking of the resurrection of Jesus? The answer would seem to be both.

Acts 1:22 tells us that the replacement for Judas was to be "ordained to be a witness with us *of His resurrection*" (Acts 1:22). How did they do this? They "preached *through Jesus* the resurrection from the dead." It is the voice of Christ that will raise the dead (see John 5:28). But Jesus didn't merely claim to be the One who will *cause* the resurrection from the dead, *He claimed to be the resurrection itself*. He said, "I am the resurrection and the life" (John 11:25).

The Well-Oiled Gate

It was the resurrection of Jesus that certified that God will judge the world in righteousness: "(God) commands all mean everywhere to repent because He has appointed a day in which He will judge the world in righteousness by that Man whom He has ordained; *whereof He has given assurance to all men, in that He has raised Him from the dead*" (Acts 17:31). We should therefore preach that all men everywhere must repent, because God has appointed a Day in which He will judge the world in righteousness. The validation that this will take place, is the reality of the resurrection of Jesus Christ. If they will obey the gospel, the risen Savior will manifest Himself to them, and confirm the fact of the Judgment.

Facial Injuries

In March of 1993, Sue and I were involved in a head-on collision. Fortunately, we sustained only minor head injuries. I was on my way back from the bathroom in the early hours of the morning when Sue got out of my side of the bed. For some reason she looked down for a second and we collided head-on, leaving us both with a fat lip. She presumed that I would see her in the dark, but I was coming from a bright light into a blackened room. I couldn't see a thing.

To presume that the unregenerate man already has the necessary light to be saved, is to come into a head-on collision with the many Scriptures which assert that there is *none* that understand (see Psalm 53:2; Romans 3:11; 8:7). If we adulterate the Word of God by making the Law invalid in its lawful use of bringing light to the sinner, we will have adulterous converts. Their hearts will love the world and the things in the world. But as we "teach all nations" and, as the disciples, cease not to "teach and preach Jesus Christ," we will see sinners come to "know His will, and approve the things that are more excellent, *being instructed out of the Law"* (Romans 2:18, italics added). The words "instructed out of the Law," suggest more than a casual reference to the Ten Commandments. To instruct out of the Law means to rightly divide the Word of Truth, as a father at the head of a table would break up bread for his children. Charles Spurgeon, in lecturing his students on evangelism, said, "Explain the Ten Commandments and obey the Divine injunction; 'Show my people their transgressions, and the house of Jacob their sins.' Open up the spirituality of the Law as our Lord did."

A well-known pastor and author once wrote an article in which he spoke of many people coming to the Savior, after he taught a series on the Ten Commandments. He said, "As a pastor I've had to come to terms with a devastating fact: Through my teaching on God's grace, an alarming number of my flock have perceived that there is nothing to learn from the Commandments now that the Law, as a schoolmaster, has gotten them to Christ. Too many view their conversion as a graduation from accountability to the Law . . . which violates Jesus' own objectives."

The man saw the consequences of an imbalance of Law and grace as being a "devastating fact." I would go further and say that what has resulted is *utterly disastrous*. These "many" (who are not confined to his church), who think they have graduated from accountability to the Law, live their lives accordingly . . . in lawlessness. They have a mere "form of godliness." They are hearers and not doers, they listen to the sayings of Jesus, but don't do them.

The direct result of the Church being confronted with biblical teaching on true and false conversion would be that the "sinning convert" would no longer be consoled in his sins. Instead of dealing with the *symptoms* of his non-account-ability lifestyle . . . his fornication, pornography, lack of discipline, lack of holiness, theft, wife beating, adultery, drunkenness, lying, hatred, rebellion, greed, etc., the counselor or pastor would deal with the *cause*. He would say, "A good tree *cannot* produce bad fruit," neither can a "fountain both yield salt water and fresh." He would gently inform his hearer: "It sounds as though you have had a spurious conversion and you need to repent of your lawless deeds, and make Jesus Christ your Lord," *using the Law of God to show the "exceeding sinfulness" of sin (Romans 7:13), and the unspeakable gift of the Cross*. This would put most Christian psychologists out of business, and cut "counseling" to a minimum.

It would also stop the insanity of modern evangelism's zeal without knowledge, because it shows that the category of "converts" who never get on fire for God, doesn't exist. There is no division in the Kingdom of God for those who are lukewarm. Jesus warned that they would be spewed out of His mouth on the Day of Judgment (see Revelation 3:16). Lukewarm "converts" are not part of the Body of Christ . . . they merely weigh heavy within the stomach of His Body until such a time as He vomits them out of His mouth. Those who entered didn't pass through the jagged-edged teeth of the Law of God. They were hard and impenitent. They were never broken by the

Law, that they might be absorbed into the bloodstream of the Body of Christ, to become His hands, His feet, and His mouth. They never felt the heartbeat of God, so their hands didn't reach out in compassion to the lost, their feet were not shod with the preparation of the gospel of peace, and their mouths didn't preach the gospel to every creature. This mass of converts are like the "backslider in heart," who is "filled with his own ways" rather than the ways of God. Their "Here I am Lord, *send him*," doesn't come from a rational fear of man, but from rebellion to the revealed will of the God they call Lord and Master.

Elisha told his servants to make some stew. However, "one went out into the field to gather herbs, and found a wild vine, and gathered from it a lap full of wild gourds, and came and sliced them into the pot of stew, though they did not know what they were." When the stew was being eaten, the guests cried out, "O man of God, there is death in the pot!" Elisha then put flour into the mixture, and "there was nothing harmful in the pot" (2 Kings 4:38-41).

The servants of the Lord have gone into the field of the world and brought back the wild vine of spurious conversions. These they added to the

Church, "though they did not know what they were." Now there is death in the pot. The answer is to add flour. Flour is flour because it has been through the process of brokenness. It has been ground to powder. The Law is the millstone that does that most necessary task.

The Wide Baby Gate

In Matthew 7:13-14, Jesus said, "Enter by the narrow gate; for wide is the gate and broad is the way, that leads to destruction, and there are many who go in by it. Because narrow is the gate and difficult is the way which leads to life and there are few who find it."

Jesus warned that the way that leads to destruction was broad. But more than that, He said it had a "gate," and that "many" would "go in" that way. If the way of destruction is the way of the world (which is the usual interpretation), why did Jesus call it a "gate" that many would "enter?" Surely if that was the case, He would rather have said that the ungodly are *born* into the way of destruction. This thought is supported by the conjunction Jesus used to join verse 13 to verse 14. He said the way of destruction is broad and many will enter into it, *because* the way which leads to life is strait and narrow. There are only two gates. If they don't go through the narrow, then they will therefore end up going through the broad. He said the wide gate is entered *because* the strait gate is narrow. If Jesus is making reference to babies being born into the broad way of destruction, why then does He *contrast* it with the narrow way which leads to life, which few will find? It seems rather that Jesus, in His usual consistency, is speaking of true and false conversion as He did in the Parable of the Sower, the wise and foolish virgins, the wheat and tares, the good and bad fish, the goats and sheep, and the wise and foolish house builders. He again uses the word "many" here in describing them, as He did when speaking of the "workers of lawlessness" He never knew.

Remember to what Jesus likened the Kingdom of God? He said, "It is like a man going to a far country, who left his house and gave authority to his servants, and each his work, and commanded the doorkeeper to watch" (Mark 13:34). The doorkeeper should keep the door. He should "watch," to only allow those who should enter to enter. Instead, we have forsaken our watch.

Acceptable Fodder

The false convert is like the Prodigal Son

before he understood that his appetites were base, that he had "sinned against Heaven" and in his father's sight. Modern evangelism fails to show him Heaven's holy standard, he doesn't see that his sin is against God, so he thinks it is quite acceptable to desire "pig food." He returns to his father, but his heart is still with the harlots. He chooses to be with the people of God, and to secretly enjoy the pleasures of sin for a season. He also finds it easier to lie (white lies) than to speak the truth, easier to steal (white-collar crime) than to pay for something, easier to lust than be holy, easier to live for himself than for others, easier to feed his mind on the things of the world rather than the things of God.

The professing convert's mind is on the things of the flesh *because he is still in the "bond of iniquity,"* as was Simon the Magician (see Acts 8:23). Like Simon, he may believe, associate with the Apostles, and see the miracles of God. He may pass through the waters of baptism, and impress many with his subtle trickery, but those who understand the Parable of the Sower and its broad implications are not swayed. They see beyond his sleight-of-hand illusion into reality. They can see, to their horror, that the Church by preaching a Lawless gospel, is ushering multitudes through Hell's broad gate . . . a gate which is oiled smooth by modern evangelism.

Nehemiah chose two men to be in charge of gathering citizens for Jerusalem. Their names were Hanani, which means *gracious*, and Hananiah, which means *Jah (Jehovah) has favored*. Scripture tells us that Hananiah was faithful and that he feared God. This was what Nehemiah charged them: "Do not let the gates of Jerusalem be opened until the sun is hot." (Nehemiah 7:2-3). God has favored humanity with the gospel of grace. Those faithful servants who fear God will seek citizens for the New Jerusalem, and they will not open the gates until the sun is hot. They will let the heat of the Law do its most necessary work.

29

The Rich Man

When non-Christians say the usual patronizing, "Well I'm sure you are happy, and that's what matters," I disagree and say I am not at all happy. I'm pleased I'm saved, but grieved that the world is not. *Do you think that the survivors of the Titanic were "happy" in the lifeboats, as their friends, loved ones, and people they didn't even know, were sinking to their deaths in those icy waters?* Should Christians, those of us who have been saved from the Titanic wrath of Almighty God, be "happy," while the icy waters of death suck our loved ones, friends, and even those we don't yet know beneath its chilling waves! The Christian will have joy unspeakable that he is saved, but like Jesus, he will be a "man of sorrows, acquainted with grief." He knows the terror of the Lord, so he persuades men.

Just a Cup

In the blackness of Adullam's cave, David longed for a drink of the cool water of Bethlehem's well. Saul hounded him like a mad dog. Dare David risk even being seen venturing outside the cave? Yet, his thirst would not die. He remembered the hot days of his childhood, when his thirst drove him to draw fresh water from the deep well. The more he thought upon it, the more his desire grew, until he broke the silence and whispered, "*Oh . . . that one would give me a drink of the water of the well of Bethlehem which is by the gate!*"

The Scriptures then tell us: "And the three mighty men broke through the host of the Philistines, and drew water out of the well of Bethlehem, that was by the gate, and took it, and brought it to David: nevertheless he would not drink thereof, but poured it out unto the Lord. And he said, Be it far from me, O Lord, that I should do this: is not this the blood of the men that went in jeopardy of their lives? Therefore he would not drink it. These things did these three mighty men" (2 Samuel 23:16-17).

The mighty three had a love for David which was more than lip-service, expressed by the fact that they risked their lives, merely to get a drink of water for their beloved leader. Their act was a display of their love. Yet, David's reaction was to pour the water out on the ground as a drink offering to the Lord.

Some may be tempted to say, "Surely, if those men went to such expense to get the water, at least David could have drunk it!" But we have here something far deeper than mere human gratitude. *David's conscience would not allow him to indulge in self-gratification.* He said, "This is the blood of the men who went in jeopardy of their lives!" *How could he drink it?* It was more than just a cup of water. It was an evident token, a symbol, proof of their love and devotion to him. The cost was too great. His only course of action was to give it to God, to pour that precious water out as a drink offering to the Lord.

One Big Gap

Sue was once awakened at 4:00 a.m. to the sound of the blaring television set. She immediately thought that one of our children couldn't sleep and they were watching TV. However, it was so loud, she decided she would go downstairs and tell them to turn it down.

When she arrived downstairs she found that one of the family dogs had accidentally stood on the remote control, and was watching the sports channel.

It fascinates us to see an animal imitate us with a wink or what seems to be a smile, or if it watches the sports channel. However, although evolution tries to link us to animals there is one big gap. As humans, we know that we are "beings." We are aware of our destiny with death. We are aware of the existence of a Supreme Being. God has placed eternity in our hearts.

A non-Christian friend of mine found he had six months to live. His friends told him to spend the last six months doing a "brothel crawl." He wasn't interested. He found that he had something within his heart considerably stronger than his sex drive . . . it was the will to live. Deep within his heart he had a cry, *"Oh, I don't want to die!"* Eternity was in his heart. Its deep whisper was, "Oh, that one would give me a drink of water from the Wells of Salvation."

Before the beginning of time, God saw not only the cry of his heart, but the cry with every human heart. The Mighty Three, the Triune God, broke through the hosts of Hell to draw water from the well of Bethlehem. God was in Christ, reconciling the world back to Himself. Now the offer to sinful humanity is: "Whosoever drinks of the water that I shall give him shall never thirst; but the water that I shall give him shall be in him a well of water springing up into everlasting life" (John 4:14).

The Bride of Christ holds the Cup of Salvation in her trembling hands. She has seen the cost of her redemption. She sees that she was not redeemed with silver or gold, but with the precious blood of Christ. Like David, she cannot drink of that cup in a spirit of self-indulgence. Rather than drink in the pleasures and the comfort of the Christian life, her reasonable service is to present herself as a living sacrifice, holy and acceptable, and pour her life out as a drink offering unto the Lord.

He's Around

I was killing time in a department store when an elderly man struck up a conversation with me. It wasn't long before the conversation swung around to the things of God. When I asked this man if he had a Christian background, his answer was interesting. He said, "Oh, I am a church-goer. I believe in God the Father; and the Son, *He's around too . . . somewhere.*" His reply was both humorous and tragic. This man went to church, obviously had faith in God, believed in the deity and the resurrection of Jesus Christ, *yet he was not saved*.

If you love God, your heart will go out to the millions who are in such a state. They are in the "valley of decision." Valleys are often without direct light, and direct light is what sinners need. They don't understand the issues. They are so close to salvation . . . it is as near as their heart and mouth. Yet without repentance, they will perish. Such thoughts are grievous. If you are born of God's Spirit, you will find that something compels you to run to the lost, to reach out to the unsaved, because God gave you a new heart that delights to do His will. The apostle Paul told of being warned by God that he would have nothing but "bonds and afflictions" in every city. Yet, he despised such afflictions, and down through the ages multitudes of Christians have followed in his steps. They were thrown to lions, burned at the stake, tortured, despised, and persecuted for their faith. Missionaries have taken the gospel to primitive heathen nations, denying themselves, putting their lives on the line. Many of them actually laid down their lives. Why do they do it, what is the compelling urge that drives them to leave the comforts of home and security of their homeland? It is nothing but the essence of the Law of God in their hearts . . . love for God and love for humanity.

The common interpretation of Hebrews 12:1 ("Wherefore seeing we also are compassed about with so great a cloud of witnesses . . . ") is that we are to run the race knowing that Moses, Abraham, Elijah, Joshua, etc., are witnesses of our race. However, another thought is that the great "cloud" is a reference to the cloud that led Israel by day (see Exodus 13:21). Just as they were to follow the cloud by day, so we are to follow the example of these men and women of faith "who have borne testimony of the Truth" (*The Amplified Bible*), and be true and faithful witnesses. The interpretation that the "witness" is their example *to* us, rather than witnesses *of* us, is also addressed by Matthew Henry. This is the day of grace. We *must* work the works of Him that sent us. The night will come when no man can work. Then, God will reveal Himself in flaming fire.

Well-known author and pastor, Oswald Chambers said, "So long as there is a human being who does not know Jesus Christ, I am his debtor to serve him until he does." Bible teacher

C.F.W. Walthers said, "A believer is ready to serve everybody wherever he can. He cannot but profess the gospel before men, even though he foresees that he can reap nothing but ridicule and scorn for it; yes, he is ready also to give his life for the gospel."

The apostle Paul said in the introduction of his letter to the Romans, that he was in debt to the world. But moral debt should not be our sole motivation. Evangelism should be an expression of gratitude to God, for who He is and what He's done. I don't know how anyone can call themselves a "Christian" and not have a concern for the lost. Charles Spurgeon said, "Have you no wish for others to be saved? Then you are not saved yourself. Be sure of that." He continued, "The saving of souls, if a man has once gained love to perishing sinners and his blessed Master, will be an all-absorbing passion to him. It will so carry him away, that he will almost forget himself in the saving of others. He will be like the brave fireman, who cares not for the scorch or the heat, so that he may rescue the poor creature on whom true humanity has set its heart. If sinners will be damned, at least let them leap to Hell over our bodies. And if they will perish, let them perish with our arms about their knees, imploring them to stay. If Hell must be filled, at least let it be filled in the teeth of our exertions, and let not one go there unwarned and unprayed for."

When an emergency vehicle drives through a city, the law demands that every other vehicle must pull over and stop. Why? *Because someone's life may be in jeopardy*. It is to be given *great* priority. That's how we should be when it comes to the eternal salvation of men and women. There is an extreme emergency. *Everything* else must come to a standstill, or we are in danger of transgressing the Moral Law, which demands, "You shall love your neighbor as yourself."

Hell should be so real to us that its flames burn away apathy and motivate us to warn the lost. Do we see the unsaved as Hell's future fuel? Do we understand that sinful humanity is the anvil of the Justice of God? Have we ever been horrified or wept because we fear their fate? The depth of our evangelistic zeal will be in direct proportion to the love we have. If you are not concerned about your neighbor's salvation, then I am concerned for yours.

The evangelistic zeal described on the previous pages should characterize a normal, biblical Christian. However, according to the *Dallas Morning News* (June 11, 1994), 68% of professing

Christians outside of the "Bible Belt" don't see evangelism as being the number one priority of the Church. Also in 1994, the Barna Research Group found that among American adults who said that they were "born again," 75% couldn't even define the Great Commission. A survey in *Christianity Today* (a major evangelistic magazine), said that only 1% of their readership stated that they had witnessed to someone "recently." That means that 99% of their readership were neither "hot" nor "cold" when it came to concern for the fate of the ungodly. They were just "lukewarm." According to *Zondervan ChurchSource, 97% of the Church has no involvement in any sort of evangelism.* Only once in Scripture did Jesus give three parables in a row. He did so to illustrate God's profound concern for the lost soul (see Luke, chapter 15).

How is it that so many who are within the Church can profess to love God, yet neglect or even *despise* evangelism? The answer is frightening.

Some years ago, I read the story that Jesus told of "Lazarus and the rich man," and interpreted it in a radically different slant than most other Christians. In fact, I have searched many commentaries, and haven't found even one which had the same interpretation. I submitted it to seven godly men. Six passed it as being sound, while the seventh wasn't too sure. I submit it to you for your consideration:

There was a certain rich man who was clothed in purple and fine linen and fared sumptuously every day. But there was a certain beggar named Lazarus, full of sores, who was laid at his gate, desiring to be fed with the crumbs which fell from the rich man's table. Moreover the dogs came and licked his sores.

So it was that the beggar died, and was carried by the angels to Abraham's bosom. The rich man also died and was buried.

And being in torment in Hell, he lifted up his eyes and saw Abraham afar off, and Lazarus in his bosom. Then he cried and said, *"Father Abraham, have mercy on me, and send Lazarus that he might dip the tip of his finger in water and cool my tongue; for I am tormented in this flame."*

But Abraham said, *"Son, remember that in your lifetime you received your good things, and likewise Lazarus evil things; but now he is comforted and you are tormented. And besides all this, between us and you there is a great gulf fixed, so that those who want to pass from here to you cannot, nor can those from there pass to us."*

Then he said, *"I beg you therefore, father, that you would send him to my father's house, for I have five brothers, that he may testify to them, lest they also come to this place of torment."*

Abraham said to him, *"They have Moses and the prophets; let them hear them."* And he said, *"No, father Abraham; but if one goes to them from the dead, they will repent."* But he said to him, *"If they do not hear Moses and the prophets, neither will they be persuaded though one rise from the dead"*
(Luke 16:19-31).

Food to the Homeless

Is this a picture of the way of salvation? If it is, then it's totally inconsistent with every other biblical reference to deliverance from death. Those who would seek to justify good works as a means of entrance into Heaven could find adequate evidence here. Let's look at the passage in the light of such a thought.

First, what was the rich man's sin? Obviously, it was failure to feed Lazarus. If that is the case, then he could have *earned* salvation. If a non-Christian wanted to earn his way into Heaven, should he then give food to the homeless? How much food would merit eternal life? No, since salvation is "by grace (Divine influence) through faith . . . not of works" (see Ephesians 2:8-9), the rich man's sin could not have been a mere failure to give Lazarus free food.

Perhaps his sin was the fact that he was rich. Then Abraham should have been damned, for he was rich. Was gluttony the rich man's sin? Not necessarily. According to, *Vine's Expository Dictionary of New Testament Words,* "sumptuously" means "goodly."

Why the reference to his clothing? Was his apparel or the color of it abhorrent to God?

Second, what did Lazarus *do* to merit salvation? Did his suffering in this life appease the wrath of God, and gain him entrance into the next? If so, then let us seek suffering instead of the Savior. Let us inflict our bodies as did the prophets of Baal, or crawl up the steps of some cold cathedral until blood pours from festered wounds, then call for the dogs to lick them. If this is a picture of the way of salvation, then Eternal Justice can be perverted, God can be bribed, and the sacrifice of the wicked is not an abomination to the Lord.

The story therefore *must* have another meaning. We will look into this in the next chapter.

30

Who is the Rich Man?

Let us establish several principles of biblical interpretation that will help us unlock the meaning of the story of Lazarus and the rich man.

1. Purple is the biblical color of royalty (see Esther 8:15).
2. Fine linen is described as "the righteousness of the saints" (Revelation 19:8).
3. The Church is referred to as the "royal priesthood" (1 Peter 2:9).
4. The tabernacle (a type of the Church) was made up of fine linen and purple (see Exodus 26:1).

It seems obvious that the rich man is what we

commonly call "the church." It is not only that great Harlot church, Babylon, who is "clothed in fine linen, purple, and scarlet" (Revelation 18:16), but also the "Bible-believing" church. The rich man is another "type" of the Harlot church we have been looking at. He is the *professing* Church, and the leper (which is what most Bible commentators agree he was) is a type of the sinner.

The foul sores of sin permeate his very being. He is as "an unclean thing." His righteousnesses are as filthy, leprous rags. They that touch him are commanded to "hate even the garment, spotted by the flesh" (Jude 1:23). Unclean spirits, like hungry dogs, feed off the wounds of his sin, waiting to consume him at death. He is laid at the gate of the church . . . that rich, fat Laodicean church . . . the "royal priesthood" of believers, clothed in fine linen and purple, faring sumptuously on the teachings of prayer, prophecy, providence, justification, sanctification, and purification. With its "abundant life" of men's camps, youth camps, marriage seminars, ladies meetings, worship, prayer, and praise; its young people's meetings, Bible studies, audio tapes, video tapes and CDs; heaping to itself teachers, having "itching ears . . . " ears so scratched by feasting, *that the muffled cries of Lazarus at the gate go unheeded!*

We have become like Israel when God said that He spoke to them in their prosperity, but they said, "I will not hear" (Jeremiah 22:21). The sin of the church isn't that it's rich, *but that it hasn't the compassion to throw even a few evangelistic crumbs to starving Lazarus at the gate.*

The rich man's thoughts are only for himself. He is filled with his own ways. We have built for ourselves big beautiful buildings, with cool clear acoustics and colorful carpets, where as cozy Christians we sit on padded pews, living in luxury while sinners sink into Hell! We say that we are rich, but we are poor, blind, wretched, miserable, and naked. I thank God for comfortable pews and quality sound systems, *but not at the expense of neglect of the lost.* We have lavished luxury on the lifeboat, while people drown en masse around us.

I have watched vast multitudes crowd around ministries of "power," "healing," and "faith," and prayed that what I suspect is untrue. I have listened to the message that these men and women bring and hoped that I was wrong in my thought that there was something radically wrong. What they say doesn't bother me, *but what is left unsaid*. There *is* healing in the atonement (who doesn't pray that God would heal a sick loved one?), we *need* to have faith in God's promises, and historically God *does* bless His people and lift them out of poverty, hunger, and suffering. *But why don't these ministers preach Christ crucified for the sins of the world?* They consistently leave the Cross out of their message, other than to mention it as the means of purchasing healing and prosperity for God's people. Why is there no preaching against sin, and exalting God's righteousness?

I look at the vast seas of people before them and think to myself that there must be many who don't know God's mercy in Christ, yet they are not warned to flee from the wrath to come. Judgment Day isn't mentioned, neither is Hell, nor is there a call to repentance. I try and be gracious and excuse them by thinking that perhaps these are "teachers" within the Body of Christ, whose particular gifting is to exhort and encourage, rather than seek to save that which is lost. However, the most gifted of teachers cannot be excused for not caring about the fate of the ungodly. The apostle Paul was the greatest of teachers, yet he pleaded for prayer that he would share the gospel with boldness, as he "ought to speak." He said, "Woe unto me if I preach not the gospel." What are the ethical implications of a fire captain who is preoccupied with making sure that his firemen are well-dressed, while people he is supposed to be saving burn to death?

I pray that the following letter I received doesn't represent the throngs who are followers of these men and women. I tremble when I suspect that it does:

> I don't think I've thanked you lately for waking me out of my false conversion. Please don't let discouragement ever hinder you from continuing to preach "Hell's Best Kept Secret." I believe it's the perfect message to wake up anyone regardless of their denomination . . . *I never, ever, thought the day would come that I would call myself an ex 'Word of Faith'er*. If Paul was a Hebrew of Hebrews, I was a faith guy of faith guys. A card carrying, tape-listening to, TV preacher watching, book-reading, seminar attending, positive confessing faith guy was I. And it was all a waste of time. I write this to show you that if one who was an extreme as myself can be snatched from such a slumber, I believe anyone with an ounce of self-honesty is a

candidate for this wake-up call. Not that I am any more opposed to the errors of Word of Faith doctrine than those of others of contemporary Christendom, but it's what I'm most familiar with. Like any of them, its greatest error is its a broad way and a wide gate.

Admirers of the Admiral

Few see how great a sin it is to neglect evangelism, because so few have any concern for the lost. Many within the Church think we are here to worship the Lord, and evangelism is for the few who have that gift. Their call to worship is a higher calling.

There was once a respectable captain of a ship whose crew spoke highly of him. They said they esteemed him to a point where everyone knew of their professed love for him.

One day, however, the captain saw to his horror that an ocean-liner had struck an iceberg and people were drowning in the freezing water ahead of his ship. He quickly directed his vessel to the area, stood on the bridge and made an impassioned plea to his crew to throw out the life-preservers. But instead of obeying his charge, the crew lifted their hands and said, "Praise the captain . . . praise you . . . we love you! You are worthy of our praise."

Can you see that the reality of their adoration *should have been seen by their obedience to his word?* Their "admiration" was nothing but empty words.

If we worship in spirit, we will also worship in truth. To lift our hands in adoration *to* God, yet refuse to reach out our hands in evangelism *for* God, is nothing but empty hypocrisy. "You shall worship the Lord your God *and Him only shall you serve*" (Matthew 4:10, italics added) is more than a mere satanic rebuke.

Those who don't have any concern for the lost may be that way because they haven't been taught biblical priority (even though it is so evident in Scripture). However, if we are aware of our debt to both Jew and Gentile, and yet refuse to hold out the Bread of Life, we prove to be part of the Harlot church. We prove to be the rich man of whom Jesus spoke.

I have always maintained that the very reason the Church exists on earth is to evangelize the world . . . to be a light in darkness, to preach the gospel to every creature. I have said that if we worship God, yet ignore His command to take the gospel to every creature, then our worship is vain. It is to draw near to Him with our lips, but to have our hearts far from Him. I have also said that if you want to find the "Evangelism Section" in your local Christian bookstore, you had better take your magnifying glass. This is not the fault of the store, but is just an indication of where the modern church's priorities lie.

With this concern in mind, I sent a manuscript of a book calling Christians back to evangelism, to an organization that reviews books to see if they are worthy of being submitted to a publisher. This is what the reviewer said:

> I like the content of this manuscript very much. It contains a much needed message for Christians about the Great Commission. Nevertheless, I see a serious problem when it comes to marketing this material. In order for a book to be marketed successfully in the bookstores, its identity must be clear. Where does this book go in the store? Is it a devotional book? Or a Bible study manual? Or is it an inspirational, 'Christian living' book?

Who is the Rich Man?

For the reason that contemporary Christian bookstores haven't a category for "evangelism," they turned it down.

The Evangelical Enterprise

One of America's most positively popular preachers once said, "I don't think anything has been done in the name of Christ and under the banner of Christianity, that has proven more destructive to human personality, and hence counter-productive to the evangelism enterprise, than the often crude, uncouth and un-Christian strategy of attempting to make people aware of their lost and sinful condition."

What then does he consider to be the "evangelism enterprise," if it's not to warn sinners to flee from the wrath to come? It is crystal clear what the problem is. Modern Christianity has degenerated into merely a means of self-improvement, self-esteem, and self-indulgence. It is self-centered rather than centered on and in the will of God. The same preacher reveals the cause of his error by saying, "The Ten Commandments were designed to put pride and dignity in your life." *That's not what the Bible teaches.* The Ten Commandments were given to do the exact opposite . . . to humble us. They show us that sin is "exceedingly sinful," and that we are in *desperate* need of God's mercy. The Bible tells us that the "Law works wrath" (Romans 4:15). It shows us the reality of God's wrath abiding on us. It is *God's* purpose for us to use the Commandments lawfully, to make people aware of their lost and sinful condition; "crude and uncouth" though it may seem to some.

Bees normally would give their lives to protect their hive, but if an intruder pumps smoke into it, they gorge themselves on honey and become lethargic, allowing their hive to be raided.

The rich man Jesus spoke of was a Jew. He called Abraham "father," and he should therefore have obeyed the Law and loved his neighbor as himself. But his love for money clouded his mind. He gorged himself on sweet prosperity, and became consumed with a self-indulgent complacency about the beggar at his gate.

Many years ago there was a doctor who was distraught at the massive death rate of mothers in childbirth. He said the answer was simply to wash the hands before assisting at births. He was ignored and even mocked in his diagnosis. *His answer was too simple*. The man was correct, but it wasn't discovered that he was right until after his death. When the medical profession put his teachings into practice, death at childbirth almost completely disappeared.

I thank God that we can stand with a diagnosed disease in one hand and a remedy in the other.

Who is the Rich Man?

The *cause* of the disease of evangelistic apathy which is so prevalent in Christendom is simply *idolatry*. This is nothing new. It was the cause of Israel's apathy towards God's Law, and the cause of her rampant history of sexual immorality (see 1 Corinthians 10:1-14). In fact, *Unger's Bible Dictionary* tells us, "The term *harlot* is used figuratively for idolatress."

A survivor of the Nazi holocaust was once asked what her terrible experience did to her belief in God. She said that it took years to come to terms with that. But now she believed that "God is loving and merciful." Then she said, "Perhaps God weeps at His inability to interfere in the works of man." A silenced Law creates an idol . . . an impotent god.

When Joash was made king, a crown was placed upon his head, and the Law of God was placed into his hand (see 2 Chronicles 23:11). When Athaliah, the daughter of Jezebel (who led Judah into idolatry, see 2 Chronicles 22:2-3), saw the young king, she cried "Treason! Treason!" The priests then charged that she be taken and executed. This was done "by the entrance of the Horse Gate into the king's house." The gate was called the Horse Gate because the "horses of the sun" were led through it for idolatrous worship (*Unger's Bible Dictionary*, p. 500).

When a person crowns Jesus as "Lord," it

means that he recognizes Him as having the Law of God in His hand . . . something utterly offensive to the Harlot church. This is because she entered by way of the Horse Gate . . . the way of idolatry.

In Luke, chapter 16, the rich man's problem was that he was idolatrous. His understanding of God was wrong. He lacked the knowledge of God, and therefore he didn't fear God, and because he didn't fear God, he didn't obey Him . . . he didn't love his neighbor as himself. Lazarus was starving at his gate, and he couldn't care less.

The irony of the story of the rich man was that he waited until he was in Hell before he became concerned for the lost. His tongue, which should have burned with zeal for the lost, burned with a tormenting and eternal thirst. The rich man and the proverbial harlot have much in common. He didn't care for Lazarus, and she didn't care for the wellbeing of the youth. All she wanted was pleasure; to feed her proud and lust-filled heart.

The *symptom* of idolatry is lawlessness within the church, and the *cure* is a correct understanding of the true nature of our Creator, revealed essentially in the Law of God. Whatever you do, *don't, like the medical profession, fall into the trap of despising the simplicity of the diagnosis.*

320

31
He Did it at Night

The answer to humanity's idolatrous plight is in Judges 6:25-27:

> The Lord said to (Gideon) "Take your father's young bull, the second bull of seven years old, and tear down the altar of Baal that your father has, and cut down the wooden image that is beside it; and build an altar to the Lord your God on top of this rock in the proper arrangement, and take the second bull and offer a burnt sacrifice with the wood of the image which you shall cut down."
> So Gideon took ten men from among his servants and did as the Lord had said to him. But because he feared his father's household and the men of the city too much to do it by day, he did it by night.

This is what happened:

1. God told Gideon to destroy his father's idols.
2. He told him to rebuild on the rock in the proper arrangement.
3. He was told to offer a sacrifice.
4. He was instructed to take ten men from among his servants.
5. He was fearful, but he obeyed.

Notice that when God commissioned Gideon, the first thing He told him to do was to destroy his father's idols. Then he was told to rebuild on the rock, in the proper arrangement. We must do the same.

With all due respect to them, I am convinced that our twentieth century spiritual forefathers (sincere though they may have been), have handed down to us an idolatrous understanding of the nature of God. We must destroy "our father's idols," then rebuild on the rock of the true character of God. To make my point, let's look at the following Scriptures, which are somewhat difficult to reconcile with the contemporary benevolent image of the character of God (italics added): "The boastful shall not stand in your

322

sight, *you hate all the workers of iniquity"* (Psalm 5:5); "The Lord will *abhor the bloody and deceitful man"* (Psalm 5:6); "The wicked boasts of his heart's desire and blesses the covetous *whom the Lord abhors"* (Psalm 10:3); "The Lord tests the righteous, but the wicked and the one who loves violence *His soul hates"* (Psalm 11:5); "*Everyone* that is proud in heart is an abomination to the Lord" (Proverbs 16:5). Contrary to modern evangelistic thinking, God does not delight in those who do evil (Malachi 2:17). In Psalm 50:22, God says He will "tear in pieces" those who forget Him. God *despises* some people (see Psalm 53:5). The Scriptures warn us that He is coming in fire, to "render His anger with fury and His rebuke with flames of fire." Whether we like it or not, our God is a "consuming fire" of burning holiness, and what's more, we have to face Him on Judgment Day.

The God of the Bible kills people. In Genesis, chapter 38, He killed a man because He didn't like what he did sexually. 1 Samuel 2:25 says of the sons of Eli, "The Lord desired to kill them." In the book of Numbers, God instructed Israel that only the Sons of Kohath were to bear the ark (in which the Ten Commandments were carried). No one else was to touch it "lest they die." Instead of doing as they were instructed, Israel put it on an ox cart, and in sincerity, with much song and dance, did it in their own way. The ox stumbled, Uzzah reached out his hand to steady the ark, and God killed him.

God said in Proverbs 1:24-26, that He would laugh and mock the ungodly when their fear comes as desolation, and their destruction comes as a whirlwind. That's hard to fit into the grinning, fat and happy, bless-me-Santa, twentieth-century-god mold.

The Lord told Israel in Jeremiah 21:5, that He would fight *against* them with an outstretched hand and with a strong arm, in anger, and in fury, and in great wrath. In 1 Samuel 6:19, He slew more than 50,000 people because they looked into the ark. The God revealed in Scripture told Joshua to kill every Canaanite man, woman, and child *without mercy*. In the Noahic flood, God killed all humanity but for eight people, solely because of their sinful thought life. Is God therefore unjust? No, "all of His judgments are righteous and true altogether." "But," you say, "all that is all Old Testament."

In the *New Testament,* God killed a man and his wife because they broke the 9th Commandment. The *New* Testament says that we should not fear him who can kill the body, but "fear Him who can kill the body and cast your soul into

Hell." The New Testament says, "Wherefore knowing the terror of the Lord, we persuade men."

True, Old Testament Law is harsh, but punishment under New Testament grace is harsher. The Bible deals out the death sentence for the first seven of the Ten Commandments . . . for idolatry, blasphemy, sabbath-breaking, parental dishonor, murder, and adultery. But the New Testament warns: "He that despised Moses' Law died without mercy . . . of how much *sorer punishment*, suppose you, shall he be thought worthy . . . who has done despite to the Spirit of grace? . . . It is a fearful thing to fall into the hands of the Living God" (Hebrews 10:28-29,31).

Despise the Law of Moses and you die without mercy. Despise the grace extended in the gospel, and your punishment will be far greater. And yet the message of the modern Church is not, *"It is a fearful thing to fall into the hands of the Living God,"* but "God loves you and has a wonderful plan for your life."

The Jesus Loves You Gospel
I have searched Scripture high and low for the "Jesus loves you" gospel, and I can't find it. If it

is there, I will gladly preach it. Nowhere can I find any of the Apostles telling sinners that Jesus loved them. The Bible does say, "For God so loved the world," but each reference to the love of God is in direct reference to the Cross (italics added):

> Herein is love; not that we loved God, but that He loved us and *sent His Son to be a substitute for our sins* (1 John 4:10).

> God commended His love toward us, in that while we were yet sinners, *Christ died for us* (Romans 5:8).

> Greater love has no man than this, *that he lay down his life* for his friends (John 15:13).

> Hereby perceive we the love of God, *because He laid down His life for us* (1 John 3:16).

> Christ also has loved us, *and has given himself for us an offering* (Ephesians 5:2).

> For God so loved the world that *He gave His only begotten Son* (John 3:16).

Where is God's Love?

How was it that the apostle Paul knew that God loved him? He was often hungry and naked. He was whipped, beaten, stoned, and so depressed that at one stage he wanted to die. He was mocked, hated, ship-wrecked, imprisoned for years, then finally martyred. What did he look to for assurance of God's love for him? He didn't look at his lifestyle because to the unlearned eye, it didn't exactly speak of God's caring hand for him. His "abundant" life was certainly full, but it wasn't full of what we think it should have been, if God loved him.

Look at Paul, lying half naked on a cold dungeon floor, chained to hardened Roman guards. Look at his bloody back, and his bruised, swollen face. "Paul, you've been beaten again. Where are your friends? Demas and the others have forsaken you. Where is your expensive chariot and your successful building program? Where is the evidence of God's blessing Paul? What's that? What did you say? *Did I hear you mumble through swollen lips that God loves you?"*

Paul slowly lifts his head. His blackened, bruised eyes look deeply into yours. They sparkle as he says two words: " . . . *the Cross!"* He painfully reaches into his blood-drenched tunic and carefully pulls out a large letter he had been writing in his own hand. His trembling and bloodstained finger points to one sentence in particular. You strain your eyes in the dim light and read, "I am crucified with Christ, nevertheless I live . . . and the life I now live in the flesh, I live by the faith of the Son of God, *who loved me and gave Himself for me"* (italics added).

Paul knew that, just as once and for all, God by creating the heavens . . . the sun, moon, stars and the sky that surrounds this massive earth . . . has displayed to humanity His incredible power, His majesty, and His glory. In the same way, so the Cross of Calvary displayed to humanity evidence of His love toward us: "But God shows and clearly proves His own love for us by the fact that while we were still sinners Christ, the Messiah, the Anointed One, died for us" (Romans 5:8, *The Amplified Bible*).

That was the source of Paul's joy, and thus his strength: "God forbid that I should glory save in the Cross" (Galatians 6:14). Those who look solely to material blessings as evidence of God's love, will think that God has forsaken them if there is a recession. But those who look to the Cross as a token of God's love, will never doubt His steadfast devotion to them.

He Did it at Night

The Cross is the show of God's love for the world. It is the focal point of our message. Calvary's Cross is the very essence of the gospel, yet I have lost count of the times I have heard gospel preachers fail *to even mention it*.

Jesus told the Pharisees that they had omitted the weightier matters of the Law, Judgment, mercy, and faith (see Matthew 23:23), and therein lies our message: there is the "proper arrangement." It is *because* of Judgment that we need mercy, and the way to obtain mercy is through faith.

So, what am I saying? I am saying that it is a grave error to tell an impenitent sinner of God's love in Christ without direct mention of the Cross. Why? *Because the Bible doesn't do so*. And how can we mention the Cross without reference to sin? And how on earth can we mention sin, without reference to the Law?

Is the sinner of today more learned than the apostle Paul who said, "I had not known sin, but by the Law?" Has God changed His mind in using the Law to "bring the knowledge of sin?" If we want to show sinners that Jesus loves them, we must do so biblically, or they will spurn His love.

We *can* evoke a tearful response by telling sinners that God loves them. It certainly is less offensive to the hearers, and therefore an easier message to give. Many years ago, before I understood the function of God's Law, I told a prostitute of God's love, and was delighted that she immediately began weeping. Unbeknown to me, her tears were not tears of godly sorry for sin, but merely an emotional response to the need of a father's love. In my ignorance, I joyfully led her in a sinner's prayer. However, I was disappointed some time later, when she fell away and became very hardened against the things of God.

32

The Devil's Pimp

I am often walking through our house in the dark of night after having a time of prayer. Past painful experiences of walking headlong into an open door have made me careful. I usually let my eyes adjust to what light there is, and even then, I safeguard myself by walking with my arms fully crossed over each other.

It's not easy to see the Harlot. Just as the true Church is hidden from the eyes of the world, so the false church is hidden from the eyes of Christians. The covering is of a "hidden spirit." Those within the Harlot's hand are like the rebellious children of Israel that took counsel, but not from God. They had a covering, but not of His Spirit, "that they may add sin to sin" (Isaiah 30:1).

The Harlot is the pride of Hell. She belongs to the Kingdom of darkness, and in darkness she is kept. But, as God has placed the iris within the natural eye which opens to accommodate light and illuminate what was before total darkness, so He can give us the spiritual eye needed to pull in light enough to see into this dark and sinister shadow. When light from Heaven shines, the harlot manifests.

There are, however, areas of the devil's dark workings which you and I can't see. The laborers could not tell the difference between the wheat and the tares. But the Bride of Heaven can "cross arms." Thanks to God, my arm can touch yours and make you aware of the Harlot, so that if we do suddenly bump into something in the darkness, we will not hit it face on and reel back in pain. We will at least be aware of what is going on. God will judge the Harlot in His time.

Meanwhile, let His still small voice guide your path to reach out to the lost. Like Elijah, who "wrapped his face in his mantle" when God spoke to him (see 1 Kings 19:11-14), the Church can hear the still, small voice of the Bridegroom, because her face is wrapped in the mantle of His holiness.

Just as Elijah cast his mantle upon Elisha to make him a new man, so Jesus cast upon penitent sinners, the mantle of the fine linen of His righteousness to make the pure, Chaste Virgin of the Church.

Then look at what happened after Elijah took his mantle and struck the water: "Now Elijah took his mantle, rolled it up, and struck the water, and it was divided this way and that, so that the two of them crossed over on dry ground. And so it was, when they had crossed over, that Elijah said to Elisha, 'Ask! What may I do for you before I am taken away from you?'

"And Elisha said, 'Please, let a double portion of your spirit be upon me'" (2 Kings 2:8-9).

Now the Church can do "greater works," because Jesus went to the Father. But more than that . . . we can now with the mantle of righteousness, strike the cold waters of death, and see them open that our feet may stand on the dry ground of everlasting life.

Driven By Her Lust

When God called Samaria a harlot (see Ezekiel 23:5), He gave her the name "Oholah." This is an obvious type of the Harlot church. The name means "her own tabernacle" (the tabernacle is a type of the Church--see Hebrews 9:11, and is called the "tabernacle of witness" in Acts 7:44).

As we have seen earlier in this book, the Samaritans were "a mixed race with a heathen core" (*Unger's Bible Dictionary*, p. 958). This was something which seems to be confirmed by Jesus, when He told His disciples to go to the Jews, but forbad them to enter the way of the Samaritans and the Gentiles (see Matthew 10:5).

Here are the accompanying signs of the harlot spoken of in Ezekiel, chapter 23:

1. She was a virgin who became a harlot (vs. 3)
2. Youths were her victims (vs. 6)
3. They were clothed with purple (vs. 6)
4. The harlot's heart was in Egypt (vs. 8)
5. She was driven by her own lust (vs. 9)
6. The cause of her sin was idolatry (vs. 30)
7. God eventually judged and exposed her for her sin (vs. 9).

As God said of Samaria: "She has never given up her prostitution brought from Egypt," so those who become one flesh with the Harlot church never find a place of repentance, because their heart is still in the world. God's fury was poured upon Samaria, and the Harlot church will one day be exposed, undone, and come under the wrath of the God she was so unfaithful to. The spurious convert's end will be like that of the idolatrous and extravagant Ahab, king of Samaria. A "certain man drew a bow at a *venture*" (which means "perfect, upright"), and struck the king of Israel between the joints of his armor ("harness" means breastplate), and as the sun was going down, he died. Then someone washed the king's chariot at a pool in Samaria, while dogs licked his blood, in "a place where harlots bathed" (outside of the city, 1 Kings 21:13,19; 22:34-38 KJV, NKJV).

This judgment is further described in Psalm 68:21-23, where God says that His judgment will fall upon the one who goes on in his trespasses: "that thy foot may be dipped in the blood of thine enemies, and the tongue of thy dogs in the same."

The false convert may fortify himself in his hypocrisy, but at the closing of time the straight and perfect arrow of God's Law will pierce his breast: "He has bent His bow, and made it ready" (Psalm 7:12). Demons will lick his blood in judgment. The stain of the sins of the Harlot will not be washed away. He will perish outside of the City of God.

May our God help us to bring the Law back

into gospel proclamation so that sinners will have the knowledge of sin and say, *"We have sinned against the Lord!"* Then slowly, it may also dawn on those who lie between the Harlot's sinful breasts in the midst of God's people, that "the harvest is passed, the summer is ended, and we are not saved." They think they know the Lord, but they don't. They are like sinful rebellious Israel in her defilement: "They do not direct their deeds towards turning to their God, for the spirit of harlotry is in their midst, and they do not know the Lord" (Hosea 5:4).

Unclean, Unclean!

If the Law is allowed to awaken them, they may hear the Word of God: "Depart! Depart! Go out from there, touch no unclean thing; *go out from the midst of her*, be clean, you who bear the vessels of the Lord" (Isaiah 52:11, italics added).

The mantle the Harlot wears as a covering is a garment spotted by the flesh. It is a defiled mantle blemished by the leprosy of sin. When an Israelite had a "bright spot . . . in the skin of his flesh, like the plague of leprosy," he was told to go to the priest for examination (see Leviticus 13:2). If the spot was leprosy, even his garments were forsaken and burned with fire (see Leviticus 13:57).

We must warn the Harlot church that her unclean covering will be examined by the High Priest of our faith. She must see that all her righteousnesses are like filthy leprous rags. We are to save them with fear pulling them from the fire, hating even the garments spotted by the flesh (see Jude 1:23). We must say with Christian, in *Pilgrim's Progress*, as he warned the hypocrite who played with sin, "Thou must forsake it then, for the Law stands at the gate and will not let one stain on thy garment pass through."

Ten Children

The Church is like Job, who had ten children who lived in harmony (see Job 1:2-4). When Satan took the ten children of the Law from her, her zeal without knowledge produced a gospel of "darkened counsel . . . words without knowledge" of the Law of her God. But when the Church, like Job, bows to the sovereignty of God and His ways, and repents in dust and ashes, God will restore her with the ten children of the Law, and will bless "the latter days more than at the beginning."

337

The Son of David

The Harlot church is like Nabal (see 1 Samuel 25:2-44). When David sent ten young men to him, saying, "Let my young men find favor in your eyes," all ten were despised:

1. Nabal was rich, like the rich man (vs. 2).
2. He was unreasonable, like those with wisdom from below (vs. 17).
3. He had sheep and goats dwelling together, like the true and false convert (vs. 2).
4. He fared sumptuously, like the rich man (vs. 36).
5. He failed to love his neighbor, like the rich man (vs. 11).
6. He was foolish (his name means "fool"), like the foolish virgins.

In contrast, the Chaste Virgin doesn't despise the Ten Commandments. They find "favor" in her eyes.

1. Both the Chaste Virgin and Abigail have the virtue of understanding (vs. 3).
2. As David sent the ten men in his own

name (vs. 5), the Chaste Virgin knows that the Law should not be separated from the Savior. They come in His Name. He came to magnify the Law and make it honorable.

3. Just as David's ten young men behaved themselves in a faultless manner (vs. 15), so the Law is without fault. It is perfect, holy, just, and good.

4. The ten young men helped to keep the sheep (vs. 16). The Virgin Church perceives that the Law continues to keep her from the power of sin as a "wall to us both by night and day." She is not a worker of lawlessness.

5. Both Abigail and the Church intercede and hold back wrath (vs. 23).

6. Each of them are of humble of heart (vss. 23-24).

7. They were once in ignorance, but now have respect for the "ten young men" (vs. 25).

8. Abigail knew that Nabal was a "son of Belial"--*son of lawlessness*, *Unger's Bible Dictionary* p.131, (vs. 25), so the Chaste Virgin knows the false convert.

9. They both call their master "lord" (vss. 26,31).

10. Like Abigail, who became united to David through marriage (vss. 40-42), so the Chaste Virgin is espoused to the Son of David, to be eventually united to Him in marriage.

Although the Church, like dull-eyed Eli the Priest cannot see that the lamp of God has gone out where the ark of the Lord is (see 1 Samuel 3:3), God is raising up children who cannot sleep. These are children who can hear the voice of God. Like Samuel, they will say, "Here I am. Speak Lord, for your servant hears." Then they will speak of that which they have seen and heard. Perhaps then, when the Church understands the lawful use of the Law, she will stop playing the devil's pimp to bring in customers for the Harlot.

33
Flashlight in the Eyes

In the mid-west of the United States, a father and two young boys waited in their car for an approaching train to pass. From his position, the driver of the train could see that the occupants were looking at something on the floor of the vehicle. To his horror, the car then slowly moved onto the tracks in front of the rapidly moving train. All three were killed.

Sadly, as they tried to retrieve whatever had fallen onto the floor, the father's foot eased off the break, and the automatic car had, evidently unbeknown to them, driven onto the tracks.

The ungodly are distracted by the deceitfulness of sin. They are about to drive onto the tracks in the face of the Justice of God. They must be awakened to see the danger. The "Jesus loves you" message of modern evangelism doesn't do that. It fails to sound any alarm.

There are clear biblical principles to help us awaken a sinner to his danger. This is why I would never begin a conversation with, "I would like to talk to you about Jesus Christ." If I want to awaken you from a deep sleep, I wouldn't put a flashlight in your eyes. That would offend you. Instead, I would use a gentle light dimmer. We do this by following the example given to us in Scripture . . . to be "gentle unto all men." We should begin in the natural realm. Why? Because, as we have also seen earlier, the natural man receives not the things of the Spirit of God, neither can he know them, they are foolishness to him because they are spiritually understood. First the natural, *then* the spiritual. We should follow the example of Jesus given to us in John, chapter 4. He began in the natural, swung to the spiritual, brought conviction using the Law, then revealed Himself to the woman at the well.

Before I understood the purpose of the Commandments, I felt like a police officer, vainly trying to coax criminals to surrender by offering them candy. Now that I have ten cannons at my command, the frustration has gone. *They come out with their hands up.* Charles Spurgeon said:

> If I just describe the Law for a moment, you will very readily see that you can never hope by any means fully to understand it. The Law of God, as we read it in the Ten Commandments, seems very simple, very easy. When we come, however, to put even its naked precepts into practice, we find that it is quite impossible for us fully to keep them . . . the Commandments, if I may so speak, are like stars. When seen with the naked eye, they appear to be brilliant points; if we could draw near them, we should see them to be infinite worlds, greater than even our sun, stupendous though it is. So it is with the Law of God. It seems to be but a luminous point, because we see it at a distance, but when we come nearer where Christ stood, and estimate the Law as He saw it, then we find it is vast, immeasurable . . . "the Commandment is exceeding broad." (*Sermons*, Seventh Series, Sheldon and Company, 1869, p. 252.)

Tombs to Their Results

Let's look back at our text in Judges 6:25-27. Gideon took "ten men from among his servants" to do what God had told him. If we desire to effectively carry out the Divine Mandate, what we must do is take the Ten Commandments and use them as our servants to bring this world to Christ. That's what they were given for, and if they will not hear Moses, neither will they be persuaded though one rose from the dead (see Luke 16:31).

We admire the good fruit of the ministries of men like George Whitefield, John Wesley, Spurgeon, and others, yet we ignore their emphasis of turning the soil of the heart with the Law before grace is presented. We build tombs to their results and prove to be murderers of their methods. In one of Whitefield's sermons, he speaks of the utter necessity of "conviction," then he says these sobering words:

> First, then, before you can speak peace to your hearts, you must be made to see, made to feel, made to weep over, made to bewail, your actual transgressions against the Law of God. According to the covenant of works, "The soul that sinneth it shall die;" cursed is that man, be he

that he may, that continueth not in all things that are written in the book of the Law to do them. We are not only to do some things, but we are to do all things, and we are to continue so to do; so that the least deviation from the Moral Law according to the covenant of works, whether in thought, word, or deed, deserves eternal death at the hand of God. And if one evil thought, if one evil word, if one evil action deserves eternal damnation, how many Hells, my friends, do every one of us deserve, whose whole lives have been one continued rebellion against God! (*George Whitefield and His Ministry*, J.C. Ryle.)

The Divided Altar

In 1 Kings, chapter 13 we read that "a man of God went from Judah (Judah means 'praise') to Bethel ('House of God') by the word of the Lord." In the House of God, King Jeroboam (whose name means "the people be multiplied") stood by the altar to burn incense. Then the man of God cried out *against* the altar and prophesied that God would raise up a king of the House of David . . . King Josiah . . . who would use the altar to destroy idolatry (see 2 Kings 23:15-16). The man then gave a sign. The altar would split apart and the ashes on it would be poured out. After that happened, Jeroboam's hand became withered and useless (see 1 Kings 13:4).

The *great multitude* making up the Harlot church stands in the *House of God* offering *praise to God*, but like Jeroboam, they are idolaters at heart. Their worship is offered on a divided altar, and, like worthless ashes, spills to the ground. The evident sign of their idolatry *is that their evangelistic hand is withered*. Their sacrifice of praise without obedience to the Great Commission is unacceptable to God. The unbending requirement for obedience is further illustrated in the same passage, when the man of God was killed for disobedience (see 1 Kings 13:21-22).

The word *withered* is "dried up" in the KJV, and means "to be ashamed." The Harlot church will lift her hands to God in worship, but is *ashamed* to reach out her hands evangelistically in service. She is ashamed to bear the reproach of evangelism in a world that disapproves of the message of the gospel.

When the man of God cried out against the altar, the king was greatly offended by his words. But the thing that helped convince him of their truth was his own withered hand.

It may seem to be blasphemous to say that worship from the "spirit-filled" church isn't acceptable to God. These are those who say they love Jesus Christ. Their altar of sacrificial praise is evident for the world to see. But look at the deathly, withered hand of the modern church. Look at it in the light of Paul's healthy outstretched hand. Compare his passion for the lost, his fear of disobedience, his moral obligation . . . *pray for me that I may speak, as I ought to speak . . . woe unto me if I preach not the gospel* . . . and you will see that the claim is not unfounded.

34

The Espoused Virgin

It must have been incredible to have been alive when Jesus walked on this earth. Sometimes the crowds were so vast, Jesus was forced out into open spaces, or had to minister from a boat, pushed out from the shore. On one of these occasions, when multitudes crowded Him, there was a woman who had suffered with internal bleeding for many years. She came up behind Him and touched the border of His garment, and was immediately healed (see Luke 8:43).

The world could offer her nothing. She had spent all her resources on medical bills, and rather than getting better, she grew worse. Her life's blood was draining from her body and there was little she could do about it. According to the Law, she had become unclean (see Leviticus 15:25), so she had nothing to lose by pushing through the crowd to touch this Man from Nazareth. But she wasn't the only one who pressed in on Him to touch the border of His garment:

> Wherever He entered, into villages, cities, or the country, they laid the sick in the market places, and begged Him that they might just touch the border of His garment: and as many as touched Him were made well. (Mark 6:56)

What was so special about the border? One answer could be that those who wanted to touch the border of the garment of Jesus, needed to stoop low to do so, significant of the humility needed before we can approach the Savior. Grace is for the humble. However, if we look at Numbers 15:38-40, we see that the border had great significance because it was there to remind the children of Israel of the Ten Commandments, and consequently keep them from harlotry.

Before the virtue of the Savior can flow into the sinner, he must be aware of the Commandments of the Lord. The effect will not only be a knowledge of sin, which will cause his hand to reach out in repentance, but it will keep him from the Harlot.

So this poor woman reached out her trembling hand and felt the hem of His garment touch her fingers. Suddenly, power flowed through her body. But it was something greater than mere "power," it was "virtue." She was more than *healed* in the normal sense of the word.

This story depicts the conversion of the true believer. Our life's blood was draining from our futile being. We were without God, without hope, and without righteousness. The Law left us wounded, bleeding, with death feeding on our malignant body. We were outcasts, aliens from the commonwealth of Israel, our garments spotted with the filth of the flesh.

Our only hope was to humbly reach out to the fine linen of the garments of Jesus Christ, and pray that somehow He could help us. Suddenly, power flowed from His body. *Power* to conquer sin, and *virtue* to cleanse us from every transgression. We were purged from the stain of the filth of the flesh . . . cleansed, sanctified, washed, purified . . . *made virgins, as though we had never defiled ourselves through sin in the first place*.

Like Ruth, we couldn't acquaint our Redeemer unless we were washed, anointed, and wearing our "best garment." We are freely given this virtue in

351

the gospel. The Church was made into a Virtuous Woman by the grace of Almighty God. This is why I think that the "virtuous woman" described in Proverbs, chapter 31, is a vivid picture of the Bride of Christ.

Careful, But Dangerous

The first admonition for the readers in this, the last chapter of the Book of Proverbs, is not to give our strength to women or to "that which destroys kings." Nor are we to give ourselves to drink wine, for "it is not for kings to drink wine, nor princes strong drink, lest they forget the Law."

The result of being drunk with natural wine is a neglect of the Law, but those who become drunk with the spiritual wine of the Harlot, those who commit fornication with her also forget the Law. The appropriate word is "antinomianism" (i.e. having no regard for the Law), something which also plagued great preachers of past centuries who longed for genuine converts.

Often drunk drivers think they are driving carefully. They drive slowly, but cross back and forth over the dividing line as they do so. They not only risk head-on collisions, but they cause people to dangerously overtake them. Their very existence is a violation of the law.

Sin deceives. It makes the Harlot church drunk with iniquity. She crosses the moral divider of the Law, using the grace of God for an occasion of the flesh. She thinks she is in a safety zone, but she is in terrible danger.

When Judah crossed the moral divider and sinned with his harlot-playing daughter-in-law (see Genesis 38:12-23), she asked for his signet, bracelets, and staff as payment for sex. The signet was a seal by which wealthy men certified legal documents. His entire wealth was dependent upon the signet. The bracelets were made of "twine-bound thread," and the staff was figurative of "the support of life, e.g., bread." These were not meant to be a permanent payment, but in his drunken passion for pleasure, Judah's thought was that he could redeem his valuables with a goat from his flock.

Tamar was really a widow and should have been clothed in the garments of her widowhood (vs. 19), but in their place wore the mantle of a harlot. Instead of redeeming the signet, the bracelets, and staff, when his daughter-in-law became pregnant because of his folly, they turned out to be the evidence of his guilt.

He who bears the name of Christ should be one whose life brings praise to God. The light of his life should shine before men that they may see his good works and glorify the Father who is in Heaven. But the hypocrite's life instead brings shame to the name of God. He joins himself to the Harlot, and as payment for the pleasures of sin, she demands his signet, bracelets, and staff. In his drunken passion for pleasure, he is deceived into thinking that the expense of the signet of the "unsearchable riches in Christ," the scarlet thread of the redeeming blood of the Savior, and the staff of the Bread of life, is merely temporary. He plans someday to redeem himself before the Day of the Lord. He thinks, like the rich man whose ground brought forth plentifully, and like the servant who thought his "Lord" delayed His coming, that he controls his own destiny. Instead, in the greatness of his folly he goes astray. The deceitful Harlot beguiles him as the serpent beguiled Eve through his subtlety. Under her alluring harlot's mantle she wears the black garments of death.

She Has Seen the Price

Then, in contrast, Scripture gives a description of the Bride of Christ in Proverbs 31:10-31, when it describes a virtuous woman:

Who can find a virtuous wife?

The Espoused Virgin

For her worth *is* far above rubies.
The heart of her husband safely trusts
her;
So he will have no lack of gain.
She does him good and not evil
All the days of her life.
She seeks wool and flax,
And willingly works with her hands.
She is like the merchant ships,
She brings her food from afar.
She also rises while it is yet night,
And provides food for her household,
And a portion for her maidservants.
She considers a field and buys it;
From her profits she plants a vineyard.
She girds herself with strength,
And strengthens her arms.
She perceives that her merchandise is
good,
And her lamp does not go out by night.
She stretches out her hands to the distaff,
And her hand holds the spindle.
She extends her hands to the poor,
Yes, she reaches out her hands to the
needy.

She is not afraid of snow for her household,
For all her household *is* clothed with scarlet.
She makes tapestry for herself;
Her clothing *is* fine linen and purple.
Her husband is known in the gates,
When he sits among the elders of the land.
She makes linen garments and sells *them*,
And supplies sashes for the merchants.
Strength and honor *are* her clothing;
She shall rejoice in time to come.
She opens her mouth with wisdom,
And on her tongue *is* the law of kindness.
She watches over the ways of her household,
And does not eat the bread of idleness.
Her children rise up and call her blessed;
Her husband *also*, and he praises her;
"Many daughters have done well,
But you excel them all."
Charm *is* deceitful and beauty is passing,
But a woman *who* fears the Lord, she shall be praised.
Give her of the fruit of her hands,
And let her own works praise her in the gates.

The Espoused Virgin

These are her qualities:

1. She is a virtuous woman (vs. 10).
2. Her husband trusts her (vs. 11).
3. She does him good (vs. 12).
4. She works willingly (vs. 13).
5. She brings food from afar (vs. 14).
6. She provides for her household (vs. 15).
7. She considers a field and buys it (vs. 16).
8. She knows her merchandise is good (vs. 18).
9. Her lamp doesn't go out (vs. 18).
10. She extends her hands to the poor (vs. 20).
11. She is not afraid of the snow (vs. 21).
12. Her household's clothed in scarlet (vs. 21).
13. She wears fine linen and purple (vs. 22).
14. Her husband is known in the gates (vs. 23).
15. She makes linen garments (vs. 24).
16. She is not afraid of the future (vs. 25).
17. She opens her mouth in wisdom (vs. 26).
18. She doesn't eat bread of idleness (vs. 27).
19. Her children call her blessed (vs. 28).
20. Her husband also praises her (vs. 28).

A "virtuous" woman literally means a wife of valor. The Hebrew word used is *chayil*, and means she has substance, wealth, valor, strength, might, and power. The word signifies a mighty army, which perfectly describes what the Church is. Her worth is far above rubies. This is evidenced by the fact that a price has been paid for her, a price greater than silver or gold . . . the precious blood of Christ.

He has extended the "border of His mantle" to cover the Church, so that He might present it to Himself a Glorious Church, not having spot, or wrinkle, or any such thing; but that it should be holy and without blemish.

Without faith it is impossible to please God. Faith and love are inseparable. If a marriage is to last, it must be built on trust: "The heart of her husband does safely trust in her" (vs. 11). This is the basis of true love. Jesus Christ has put us in trust with the gospel, even so, we speak not as pleasing men, but God Who tries our hearts. This is why we must not betray that trust, by either adding to His Word, or by diminishing it. The love the Husband has for the spotless Bride of Christ is seen in the Song of Solomon: "Thou art all fair, my love; there is no spot in thee." (KJV)

The day of my daughter's wedding, I rounded a corner with her on my arm. Suddenly, hundreds of people stood to their feet. I have preached before thousands, but the sight of so many people turning at once, and hearing dozens of cameras clicking, almost made my knees go weak.

After the wedding I asked Rachel what she thought of the traumatic experience. She said that she didn't notice anyone. *She had her eyes solely on the groom.*

Therein is the key to attractions and distractions of this world. Whether the world stands to their feet to applaud her good works, or picks up stones to kill her for the gospel's sake, the Bride of Heaven hardly notices them. Her eyes are on Jesus, the author and finisher of her faith. Like Stephen, she sees Jesus, standing at the right hand of God.

35

Super Bowl Sunday

I was a little tired as I boarded a flight from Dallas to Los Angeles, so I requested three seats in a row. It was Superbowl Sunday, so the flight was fairly empty. I was therefore able to gather six or seven blankets and six pillows to make myself a bed. Then I sat back in ease and comfort.

Suddenly, I saw a young couple with a scream-machine two seats in front of me. I have been on flights where the baby screamed louder than the engine of a 747 at full throttle for what seemed hours, so I gathered up my blankets and pillows and quickly moved down to the back of the plane.

Then I watched in horror as the couple gathered all *their* belongings, including their offspring, and also moved to the back of the plane. They were fully aware of the potential disturbance in their arms, and had moved down to the rear of the plane so as not to trouble other passengers. As they laid out their belongings on the seats, I casually gathered my bedding and went back to my seat. It was so obvious that I was trying to get away from the baby that was following me. In fact, the husband called out, "I see you're trying to get away from the baby. *I wish I could join you!*"

Every Christian has a plane-baby that follows him through life. The baby's name is Tribulation. We may try and keep at a distance, but that baby is sent from God to "stablish, strengthen, and settle us." The winds of adversity help a tree that is planted on good soil. The Christian grows stronger in fiery trials. The Chaste Virgin understands this and has faith in God's ability to work good out of evil. When tribulation strikes her, she doesn't lift a sinful fist at the heavens. She lifts up holy hands and offers the sacrifice of praise. She allows trials to purify her. She bows to the sovereignty of her Lord, and eagerly awaits His coming.

Her love for Him is seen in that she delights to do His will. When she does a good deed for a stranger, it grieves her if the person doesn't know that she is espoused to Christ, and that her motivation is solely for God's glory. Her soul makes her boast in the Lord. What's more, she will only want "to do him good, and not evil, all the days of her life" (Proverbs 31:12). The true convert says, "For to me to live is Christ, and to die is gain." She lives only for her Husband.

The Bible then tells us this virtuous woman "works willingly with her hands" (vs. 13). True Christians are laborers, always abounding in the work of the Lord, for they know that their labor is not in vain. They are prepared to get their hands dirty, to sweat for the Lord, to go to the highways, the byways, and the hedges. They are energized by gratitude, because they see the fathomless love of God demonstrated at the Cross. They understand that salvation was all of grace, and therefore present their bodies as living sacrifices, holy and acceptable to God, which is their reasonable service.

I once bought an anniversary card for Sue which so expressed how I felt about her, I almost wept when I gave it to her. It said, "It only takes a moment to say 'I love you;' but it will take a lifetime to show it."

That's how the Bride of Christ feels about her Husband. And when it is all done she will say that we are unprofitable servants . . . we have done that which was our duty to do.

The true Church "brings food from afar off" (vs. 14), and "rises while it is yet night, to give food to her household" (vs. 15). She knows that she must get the manna from Heaven. She lives not by bread alone, but by every Word that comes from the mouth of God. She has meat to eat that the world knows nothing of. She makes sure that not only the lambs and sheep within the Church are fed, but also the children of her household. God has given her the gift of children and therefore she is quick to obey the command to "train up a child in the way he should go, so that when he is old, he will not depart from it." She doesn't shift the responsibility solely to a Christian school or to Sunday School, but establishes the altar of family devotions within the home, bringing them up in the admonition of the Lord. This means teaching her children the Law, in all its strictness.

The Bride of Christ "considers a field," and "plants a vineyard" (vs. 16). She is very concerned about reaching the lost, and then establishing them in the vineyard of the local church. She *considers* the field of the world . . . their terrible fate. She ponders ways and means of reaching them. Her prayers are not prayers of self-indulgence, but come from a burden to touch lives in the name of Jesus Christ. Her chief aim is to warn every man that she may present every man perfect in Christ Jesus.

She "girds her loins with strength" (vs. 17), because she knows that if she is not strong in the Lord and in the power of His might, the enemy will hinder her labor in the gospel. She "perceives that her merchandise is good; and her lamp goes not out at night" (vs. 18). The English language understates what great treasure we have in earthen vessels. *We have found immortality! Our merchandise is good in the truest sense of the word!* Who in the human race could have ever dreamed of what we have found in Jesus Christ?

We are not as the foolish virgins who let their lamps go out. We keep ours trimmed and ready because we are looking for the coming of the Bridegroom. We know that the day is nearing when the heavens will roll back as a scroll when it is rolled together, and we will see Him in His glory. We will say, "This is our God . . . we have waited for Him!" What a day of unspeakable joy, when death shall forever be swallowed up in victory, but what a fearful day for the ungodly. They will flee to the rocks and the mountains, and cry for the rocks to fall on them, and hide them from the face of Him who sits on the throne and from the wrath of the Lamb.

The Virgin of Jesus Christ "stretches out her hands to the poor; yes, she reaches out her hands to the needy" (vs. 20). She is "careful to maintain good works." How can we say we are part of the Bride of Christ, and say, "God bless you . . . be warmed and filled," and not give them "those things which are needful to the body"? If we don't care about the poor and the needy, then we don't love our neighbor as ourselves, and we therefore have no basis to say that we are saved. If we don't have love, then we don't have God: "He that loves not knows not God; for God is love."

Arm's Length

Sue had been visiting an elderly woman in a convalescent home, and had mentioned that there was another woman in her room named "Stanka." She said that this rather large foreign woman was angry, foul-mouthed, and very blasphemous.

One day I went with Sue to see the elderly woman. Stanka had never seen me before, but as soon as she laid her eyes on me, her first words to me were, "Come here. *I'm going to punch your nose!*"

On the day our elderly friend left the home, I wheeled another lady around the wards in her wheelchair. She said that her family had abandoned her, so two days later I took her some flowers. But when I inquired as to her whereabouts, I found that they had taken her to another convalescent home, so I decided to give the flowers to Stanka.

I found her, placed the flowers in her lap, (keeping my nose at arm's length) and said, "These are for you." Her eyes widened, and she actually smiled. We then went into her room and I put them into a vase. She let me give her one of our gospel tracts, and even thanked me.

The way to a woman's heart is through someone else's flowers.

For the Christian, good works are a pure fragrance for us to place in the lap of the ungodly. They defuse the enmity against God and His Law. They "put to silence the ignorance of foolish men."

Neither is the Church "afraid of the snow for her household" (vs. 21). The cold snow of the trials, temptations, and persecutions still come, but she has faith in God. The Virtuous Woman knows that God will never leave nor forsake her. The reason for this is that "all her household are clothed with scarlet" (vs. 21). She knows that the scarlet of the tabernacle is a type of the blood of Jesus. It is the blood of the Savior that makes her acceptable, pure, full of virtue, and completely blameless in the sight of her Lord. It's the blood that means all of God's promises of care and providence are now to her "Yea and Amen."

The Church's mantle is one of "fine linen and purple" (vs. 22), the color of royalty. Her husband is the King of Kings who has clothed her in a priestly garment of righteousness.

Keeping the Garment Unblemished

The man who previously owned our home put eight lights above one of our bathroom mirrors. These lights are regulated by a dimmer. Each day I have the choice of having them on full strength, and gazing at the harrowing sight of wrinkles, spots, blemishes, and thinning hair. Or I can deceive myself by having the lights dimmed. When they are turned down, my hair looks thick and my skin looks smooth. *This makes me feel better about myself.*

When James 1:25 talks about looking into the "perfect Law of Liberty," the Bible is speaking of the Ten Commandments. This is clear from the context of Scripture (see James 2:9-10). All New

Testament ethical admonition traces its roots to the moral Law of God. When we look into God's mirror . . . the "perfect Law of Liberty". . . we have a choice. We can have the light of conscience on full strength, or we can dim it a little. *This will make us feel better about ourselves*.

Let's surmise that I borrowed $15 off Fred Smith two years ago. Even though I said I would pay him back within two weeks, I haven't done so. When I look into the Law and see, "Thou shalt not steal," I can dim the light by saying, "That was two years ago . . . he's probably forgotten." That may be true. Fred may have forgotten, but God hasn't. I have stolen Fred's money, and the Law says, "Thou shalt not steal." I have broken the Eighth Commandment. I have lied to him, and broken the Ninth. I have dishonored the good name of my father and my mother and broken the Fifth, by being a lying thief. If Fred does remember, I am causing God's name to be blasphemed because of my hypocrisy, and have broken the Third. I have not loved my neighbor as myself, by lying to and stealing from him. My actions have revealed that I don't love God with all of my heart, mind, soul, and strength, and I have therefore transgressed the essence of the Law. I have broken the First Commandment by not putting God first. I have loved money more than God. I have broken the Second Commandment with idolatry. My god is actually an idol, who doesn't mind iniquity.

I may feel good about myself in the darkness of a seared conscience, but the day will come when I shall be judged by the brilliant light of the Law of the Lord (see James 2:12). The Scriptures say, "Blessed are the undefiled in the way, who walk in the Law of the Lord. Blessed are they that keep His testimonies and that seek Him with the whole heart. *They also do no iniquity*: they walk in His ways" (Psalm 119:1-3, italics added, KJV). The Chaste Virgin lives *for* and *by* righteousness.

May the fear of God awaken those whose conscience has lost its life. May the Law drive them to the Cross, because Jesus is coming for a perfect Church, without spot, wrinkle, or blemish. God is not willing that they perish. Mercy rejoices over judgment. For "there is one Law-giver, who is able to save and to destroy" (James 4:12).

Fine Linen

The virtuous woman's husband is also "known in the gates" (vs. 23). The gates of Hell tremble at the very name of Jesus Christ, because God has given Him a name that is above every name, and every knee will bow before Him. He holds the keys to death and Hell. He has all authority in Heaven and in earth . . . and He has given it to His espoused. He has trusted her with the door keys (see Matthew 16:19).

The Bride of Christ also "makes fine linen and sells it" (vs. 24). She knows that her supreme object is to cover sinners in robes of righteousness, so, like Lydia, she is a "seller of purple." She also knows that without the fine linen of the mantle of the righteousness of the saints, she and her household would perish.

It is the Church that "opens her mouth with wisdom . . . and eats not the bread of idleness" (vss. 26-27). She confines her counsel strictly to the bounds of the Word of God, redeeming the time for the days are evil, always abounding in the work of the Lord. She has gone to the ant and considered her ways. She has the mind of Christ and the wisdom of the Word of God at her fingertips.

Then the Scriptures say, "Her children rise up and call her blessed, and her husband also praises her" (vs. 28). How many of those who once called themselves "children of the Lord," but have turned their backs on Him, call the Church "blessed?" In my experience, the end products of modern evangelism despise the Bride of Christ and curse her. They see the Bride as a "savior of death unto death," and they themselves become disillusioned and bitter.

How incredible it is that the Lord can "praise" the Church. The Chaste Virgin, like the virtuous woman is a crown to her husband (see Proverbs 12:4), but she that makes ashamed is as rottenness in his bones. Those who truly love Him, tremble at His Word and handle it with fear: "Favor is deceitful, and beauty is vain: but a woman that fears the Lord, she shall be praised. Give her of the fruit of her hands; and let her own works praise her in the gates" (vss. 30-31).

She came through the shed blood of the Savior, not as Cain. Her works followed her. Those who flee to Jesus Christ to escape the thunderings of the Law, rise up and call her "blessed." They know that those who trust in the cleansing power of Jesus Christ, have the blessing of their Lord. She, like Solomon's dove, remains faithful for life. The Bride can look forward to hearing words of praise from the lips of her husband, "Well done, you good and faithful servant."

36

The Consummation

The Chaste Virgin has been cleansed of her sin. She greatly rejoices in the Lord. Her soul is joyful in her God, because He has clothed her in the garments of salvation. He has covered her with the robe of righteousness as a bridegroom decks himself with ornaments, and as a bride adorns herself with jewels (see Isaiah 61:10). The time will come when she will therefore be freely given pleasures forevermore. She will be brought out as a bride, glorified in the wedding garments of pure white righteousness (see Romans 8:17,30). She says, "He will bring me forth to the light, and I will see His righteousness" (Micah 7:9).

The Harlot, however, will be stripped of her deceptive mantle, exposing her shame. The Virgin Bride will say, "Then she who is my enemy will see, and shame will cover her who said to me, 'Where is the Lord your God?' My eyes will see her; now she will be trampled down like mire in the streets" (Micah 7:10).

The Espoused Virgin will no longer be a virgin when her Bridegroom comes. Her every desire will be satisfied through a consummate union with Him (see Revelation 22:17).

In Deuteronomy 22:15-21 the Bible says that there should be evidence of a virgin bride. If there was no evidence that she was a virgin, she was to be taken to the door of her father's house and stoned to death "because she played the harlot in her father's house."

The evidence that the Bride of Christ is a chaste virgin is the blood. She is pure because of the blood of the New Covenant. The life of her flesh is in the blood. It cleanses her from all sin. When God looks upon her, He sees the blood and His wrath passes over her. She has applied the blood to the door posts of her house.

When those who profess to be the Virgin Bride are found to be without the blood, the stones of God's Law will fall upon them and grind them to powder . . . because they "played the harlot in the House of the Lord."

The Harlot church will never find consummation. She will thirst forever, and cry out in torment for a drop of water to cool the flame on her godless tongue. It was once metaphorically a "fire, a world of iniquity . . . set on fire by Hell," but now it is literal. She can't complain, however, because she is only being paid in full for her iniquity . . . *the Law will make sure of that*. The wages for her sin will be death. She could have inherited the endowment of her God. . . pleasure forevermore . . . the gift of eternal life through Jesus Christ our Lord. But she didn't make Him her Lord. The mantle of sin's deceit blinded the Harlot's own evil eyes. She will be destroyed through lack of knowledge of the Law of her God. She was never given that knowledge.

Tell me . . . *on whom does the guilt rest?*

* * *

Epilogue:

I received the following letter from a pastor in Arizona, in September 1996:

Pastoring the same flock for over 18 years, I had almost reached the conclusion I would never enjoy much evangelistic fruit from my preaching (or the ministry of our church). We had seen lots of transfer growth over the years but very little conversion growth, and my heart *ached* to hear the 'cries of the newborn.' Many times I contemplated leaving the ministry altogether because I wanted so badly to see God's Kingdom expand through our labors. One wall in our prayer room is called the 'Wailing Wall,' the other the 'Victory Wall.' After one whole year there was only *one* name transferee to the Victory Wall.

But in God's awesome timing I was exposed to (the use of the Law in evangelism) only weeks before our first 'month of Seeker Services.' We are not a Seeker Church but we decided to hold a month of services aimed at the seeker, in which each sermon would address the Word to both the believer and the non-believer. The first Saturday night only 5 'seekers' were even in the service--I could recognize just about everyone else. But that was to change. One young man, after hearing the Law of God preached and watching the 'tutor draw men to Christ,' went home and invited a number of his relatives and brought them back Sunday morning. *The next morning I saw the greatest work of God in our church I've ever seen.* To God be the glory. That morning over 20 people indicated their desire to be baptized. And the story is not yet over. As I hurriedly finish typing this report, I am preparing to run off to an appointment with a father whose wife was baptized last week. After hearing the Law of God preached, he broke down in tears and wants to follow his wife in the waters of Baptism. To God be *all* the glory. **Pastor Nathan Lutz, Phoenix, Arizona**.

We have tapes, videos, books (including exciting new publications), and unique tracts by Ray Comfort to help you be more effective in your witness. You may like to purchase our 16 tape series (pictured). When you buy this, we will give you five of Ray's books, free of charge.

377

Write or call for an up-to-date list of all of our products (or send $4.50 for a sample of all of our unique tracts).

Hundreds of churches and individuals have purchased our "Excellence in Evangelism" video series ($99.95 plus $6 S/H--money back if not delighted). When you buy these videos, we will give you ten titles of our books--free of charge.

The series contains ten different teachings by Ray Comfort, averaging 50 minutes each: Hell's Best Kept Secret, How to Witness Effectively, How to Obtain Zeal, True and False Conversion, and six other eye-opening teachings to thoroughly equip you for effective evangelism. See below for ordering details.

Living Waters Publications
P.O. Box 1172
Bellflower, CA 90706, U.S.A.

Phone (310) 920 8431, Fax (310) 920 2103, or order
by credit card 1(800) 437 1893. Please note: our area
code will change to (562) early in 1997. Visit our Web
Page: http://metanet.net/comfort